Insert Module
Menu Editor
Object Browser

Toggle
Breakpoint
Instant Watch

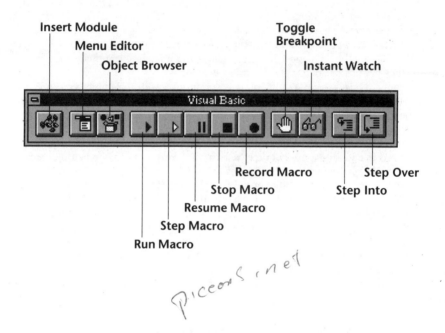

Record Macro
Stop Macro
Resume Macro
Step Macro
Run Macro

Step Over
Step Into

Piceons.net

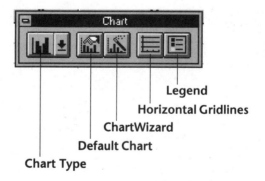

Legend
Horizontal Gridlines
ChartWizard
Default Chart
Chart Type

For every kind of computer user,
there is a SYBEX book.

All computer users learn in their own way. Some need straightforward and methodical explanations. Others are just too busy for this approach. But no matter what camp you fall into, SYBEX has a book that can help you get the most out of your computer and computer software while learning at your own pace.

Beginners generally want to start at the beginning. The **ABC's** series, with its step-by-step lessons in plain language, helps you build basic skills quickly. Or you might try our **Quick & Easy** series, the friendly, full-color guide.

The **Mastering** and **Understanding** series will tell you everything you need to know about a subject. They're perfect for intermediate and advanced computer users, yet they don't make the mistake of leaving beginners behind.

If you're a busy person and are already comfortable with computers, you can choose from two SYBEX series—**Up & Running** and **Running Start**. The **Up & Running** series gets you started in just 20 lessons. Or you can get two books in one, a step-by-step tutorial and an alphabetical reference, with our **Running Start** series.

Everyone who uses computer software can also use a computer software reference. SYBEX offers the gamut—from portable **Instant References** to comprehensive **Encyclopedias**, **Desktop References**, and **Bibles**.

SYBEX even offers special titles on subjects that don't neatly fit a category—like **Tips & Tricks**, the **Shareware Treasure Chests**, and a wide range of books for Macintosh computers and software.

SYBEX books are written by authors who are expert in their subjects. In fact, many make their living as professionals, consultants or teachers in the field of computer software. And their manuscripts are thoroughly reviewed by our technical and editorial staff for accuracy and ease-of-use.

So when you want answers about computers or any popular software package, just help yourself to SYBEX.

For a complete catalog of our publications, please write:

SYBEX Inc.
2021 Challenger Drive
Alameda, CA 94501
Tel: (510) 523-8233/(800) 227-2346 Telex: 336311
Fax: (510) 523-2373

SYBEX is committed to using natural resources wisely to preserve and improve our environment. As a leader in the computer book publishing industry, we are aware that over 40% of America's solid waste is paper. This is why we have been printing the text of books like this one on recycled paper since 1982.

This year our use of recycled paper will result in the saving of more than 15,300 trees. We will lower air pollution effluents by 54,000 pounds, save 6,300,000 gallons of water, and reduce landfill by 2,700 cubic yards.

In choosing a SYBEX book you are not only making a choice for the best in skills and information, you are also choosing to enhance the quality of life for all of us.

The Up & Running Series from SYBEX

Other titles include Up & Running with:

AutoSketch 3

Clipper 5.01

dBASE III PLUS

DOS 5

DOS 6

DOS 6.2

Flight Simulator

Harvard Graphics 3

Harvard Graphics for Windows

PROCOMM PLUS 2.0

Window 3.1

Word 6 for Windows

Word for Windows, Version 2.0

WordPerfect 5.1 for DOS

WordPerfect 5.1 for Windows

WordPerfect 6 for DOS

WordPerfect 6 for Windows

XTree Gold 2

Up & *Running*

with Excel 5
for Windows™

Sheila S. Dienes

SYBEX®

San Francisco • Paris • Düsseldorf • Soest

Acquisitions Editor: Rudolph S. Langer
Developmental Editor: Richard Mills
Editor: David Krassner
Technical Editor: Maurie Duggan
Production Editor: Carolina Montilla
Production Artist: Helen Bruno
Screen Graphics: Cuong Le
Typesetter: Ann Dunn
Proofreader/Production Assistant: Sarah Lemas
Indexer: Liz Cunningham
Cover Design: Archer Design

To Jean Scott

··· Acknowledgments

Many people are involved in the production of a book, and this one is no exception. Special thanks to David Krassner, editor, whose insights and good humor helped ease the task. To Maurie Duggan, technical editor, my gratitude for pointing the way. Contributions from Carolina Montilla, production editor, Cuong Le, screen graphics, Ann Dunn, typesetter, Helen Bruno, artist, and Sarah Lemas, proofreader, were invaluable.

My heartfelt thanks to Richard Mills, developmental editor, who offered me the opportunity to write the book.

$\cdots$ **Table of Contents**

· · · **Preface**

Microsoft Excel for Windows is one of the most popular
spreadsheet programs available. It is more than a powerful,
easy-to-use spreadsheet program, though, because it contains
both charting and database capabilities.

The newest version of Excel combines many of the features
of previous versions with accessible commands on toolbars and
shortcut menus, improved dialog boxes, and *Wizards* to lead you
step by step through a task. In addition, the default in Excel 5
is the *workbook*, a group of individual worksheets. Excel automatically saves worksheets of related data in the same file.

· · · **How This Book Is Organized**

This book is designed to introduce you to Excel 5, whether you
are new to spreadsheets, new to Excel, or upgrading from a
previous version of Excel. There are 14 chapters in the book.
No chapter will take longer than 15 minutes for you to read
and follow the included steps. The early chapters focus on the
basics of creating a worksheet, and later chapters progress
through working with a database and creating a chart. You
needn't read the chapters in order.

... Conventions Used in This Book

To make your reading easier, the following conventions are used in this book:

Fast Track   Each chapter includes a *Fast Track* list at the beginning. Glance at the list when you want a quick reminder of how to accomplish a task described in the chapter.

Menu commands   Commands you can access from the menu bar appear as *Menu* ➤ *Command*. If the command has a shortcut key sequence, it appears in parentheses in bold lettering after the command. For example, if we say "select File ➤ Save (**Ctrl+S**)" it means "pull down the File menu and choose Save, or press and hold **Ctrl**, then type **S** and release both keys."

Select   Highlight data in worksheet cells, or choose a dialog box option. When data is highlighted, it appears in reverse video.

Click   Press and quickly release the left mouse button.

Double-click   Rapidly click the left mouse button twice in succession.

Right-click   Press and quickly release the right mouse button.

Drag   Click and hold the left mouse button, and move the mouse until the data or object is selected. Then release the mouse button.

Select a check box   Click on a check box to "turn on" its corresponding option. A selected check box contains an *X*.

Clear a check box   Click on a check box to "turn off" its option and remove the *X* from the box.

Preview   Many dialog boxes contain an area that displays how a sheet will appear with options you select.

Getting Started

IN order to run Excel, you must have Windows running. To
run Windows, type **win** and press ↵ at the C:\> prompt. When
the Program Manager appears on your screen, you can start
Excel, as described next.

••• Starting Excel

When the Program Manager appears on your screen, double-click on the Microsoft Office icon to open the group window that contains Excel. Then double-click on the Microsoft Excel icon shown in Figure 1.1.

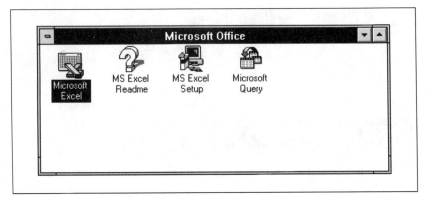

FIGURE 1.1: *The Microsoft Excel icon*

••• The Opening Screen

Each time you start Excel a new *workbook window* appears on your screen. Figure 1.2 shows a workbook window with the parts of the window labeled.

 *When we want you to choose a menu command, we will follow the convention* menu ➤ command.

You can also open a new workbook window while you are working in Excel. Click on the **New Workbook** button on the Standard toolbar or choose File ➤ New (**Ctrl+N**), then choose **OK**.

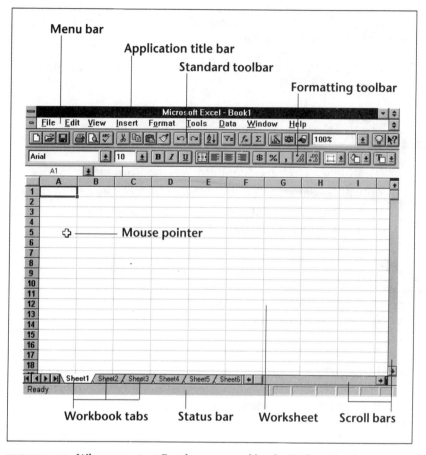

FIGURE 1.2: *When you start Excel, a new workbook window appears.*

The Workbook Window

Figure 1.2 shows several elements that make up a workbook window.

> **Title bar**   The title bar tells you the name of the active window. The title bar at the top of the screen indicates the application window. The "Book 1" title bar indicates the active workbook window.

Maximize the workbook window to display more of the active worksheet.

Menu bar   Each menu on the menu bar contains related commands.

 *Many of the menu commands also have* hot *key combinations, a single shortcut key, or a key sequence.*

Toolbars   Both the Standard and the Formatting toolbars appear by default on your screen. Use your mouse to click on the toolbar buttons. When you point to a button, its function appears in a *ToolTip*.

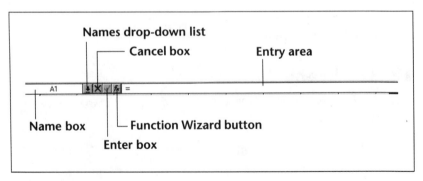 *Shortcut menus are available for most tasks. To access a shortcut menu, move the mouse pointer to a selection or cell and click the right mouse button. Then click on the command you want to use in the shortcut menu.*

Formula bar   The formula bar is activated when you begin to type in Excel. The data you type appears both in the cell and in the formula bar. The formula bar contains several components, shown in Figure 1.3.

FIGURE 1.3: *The parts of the formula bar*

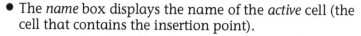

- The *name* box displays the name of the *active* cell (the cell that contains the insertion point).
- Click on the *names* drop-down list button to display a list of cell or range names in the current workbook.
- Click on the *cancel* box to deactivate the formula bar without changing the contents of the active cell.
- Click on the *enter* box to replace the contents of the active cell with the data in the formula bar.
- Click on the *Function Wizard* button to display the Function Wizard dialog box.
- When the formula bar is active, data you enter appears in the *entry* area.

Worksheet   The workbook window contains a worksheet, which is made up of a grid of lettered columns and numbered rows. At the intersection of each column and row is a *cell*.

 *There are 256 columns (which contain the column headings A through IV) and 16384 rows in a worksheet.*

Data you enter in worksheet is entered directly into a cell. Cells are defined, or *referenced*, by the column letter and row number. For example, the cell at the intersection of column C and row 4 is called C4.

Workbook tabs   The name of each sheet in the workbook appears on the workbook tabs. The name of the active worksheet appears in **bold** characters.

Scroll bars   The workbook window contains both a horizontal and a vertical scroll bar.

Status bar   The status bar displays information about the current task, command, or toolbar button.

Mouse pointer The mouse pointer changes its appearance according to the task it is performing. When it is in the worksheet's grid, it appears as a three-dimensional plus sign.

••• Selecting Items in the Worksheet

To enter data into a cell or perform an action on any data, you must first *select* the cell or data. Data that is selected appears in reverse video.

To select a cell, move the mouse pointer over the cell then click the left mouse button. The cell appears with a thick border and has a small black square, called a *handle*, at its lower-right corner. In Figure 1.4, cell B3 is selected.

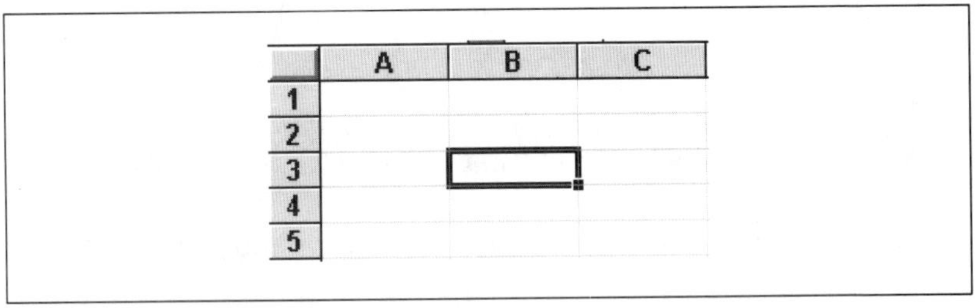

FIGURE 1.4: *Cell B3 is selected.*

If you want to select a *range* (more than one adjacent cell), click on the top-left cell of the range, then drag the mouse down and to the right. A range is defined by the references of its first and last cells, separated by a colon (:). For example, in Figure 1.5, the range C3:D5 is selected.

NOTE *Notice that the first cell in the range appears with a border instead of in reverse video. Any data you enter will be placed in the cell with the border.*

	A	B	C	D	E
1					
2					
3			6	7	
4			8	9	
5					

FIGURE 1.5: *The range C3:D5 is selected in the worksheet.*

Figure 1.5 shows how cells and data appear when they are selected. To select non-adjacent cells or ranges in a worksheet, press the **Ctrl** key while you click or drag.

Click on the *column heading* (the gray area around the column letter) to select the entire column. Click on the *row heading* (the gray area around the row number) to select the entire row.

· · · Moving around the Worksheet and Workbook

To move through a worksheet or to a different worksheet in your workbook:

- Drag one of the scroll boxes to move to a general area of the worksheet.
- Click on one of the scroll buttons to move the part of the worksheet that appears on your screen one row up or down, or one column left or right.
- Press ↑, ↓, ←, or → to move one cell up, down, left, or right.
- Press **Ctrl+End** to select the last cell in the worksheet that contains data.
- Press **Ctrl+Home** to move to the first cell in the worksheet.
- Press **Home** to move to the beginning of the row.

- Click on the vertical scroll bar or press **Page Up** or **Page Down** to move one screen up or down, and on the horizontal scroll bar to move one screen left or right.

- Click on the sheet tab, or press **Ctrl+Page Up** to move to the previous sheet or **Ctrl+Page Down** to move to the next sheet in a workbook.

- Click on the name box on the formula bar, then type the cell reference or range name to which you want to move and press ↵.

... Getting Help

Online Help is always available in Excel. To access Help:

- Click on the **Help** button on the Standard toolbar, then click on the command or item for which you want help.

- Press **F1** when the command or item you want help with is highlighted.

- Double-click on the **Help** button to open the Search dialog box, and begin typing a keyword in the text box. As you type, the highlight moves to the nearest item that matches your text. Select Show Topics (**Alt+S**) to display topics related to the keyword. Click on the topic or press ↑ or ↓ to highlight it, then select **Go To** (**Alt+G**).

- Click on the button or press **Alt+H** to display help for a dialog box.

- Click on the "lighted-up" **TipWizard** button on the Standard toolbar to display tips on using Excel.

- Choose Help ➤ Examples and Demos, then select a topic to see step-by-step instructions for completing a task.

Creating a Workbook

YOU can enter data in the form of text, numbers, and formulas into a worksheet or automatically enter a series of data with AutoFill. Always select the cell where you want to place your data.

••• Entering Numbers in a Cell

Type the number then press ↵ to enter the number into the cell and activate the next cell in the column. Numbers are right-aligned within the cell (they appear along the right edge of the cell).

••• Entering Text in a Cell

Select the cell in which you want to place text, then type other characters or numbers. Press ↵ to enter the text in the cell and activate the next cell. The text you entered is left aligned in the cell (it is aligned along the left edge of the cell).

••• Entering Dates and Times

Dates and times are actually numbers in Excel. Excel stores dates as serial numbers and times as decimal fractions, so you can calculate dates and times in a worksheet. Dates and times are automatically formatted in one of several styles.

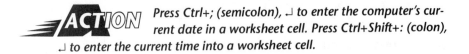 *Press Ctrl+; (semicolon), ↵ to enter the computer's current date in a worksheet cell. Press Ctrl+Shift+: (colon), ↵ to enter the current time into a worksheet cell.*

••• Using AutoFill to Enter Data

Use AutoFill to enter an incremental series, to copy data, or to extend data adjacent to cells that contain data.

Excel sometimes recognizes text in a single cell as the beginning of a series. Follow these steps to create a series:

1. Enter **January** in cell A1. Excel identifies that data as part of a sequence.

2. To extend the series, click on cell A1 and then move the mouse pointer to its *fill handle*, the small black square at the lower-left corner of the cell. The mouse pointer appears as a two-dimensional plus sign.

3. Drag the fill handle to the right, across cells B1, C1, D1, and E1. As you drag, a crosshatched border appears around the cells in the selection.

4. Release the mouse button. Each cell in the selection is automatically filled with *February, March, April,* and *May,* as shown in Figure 2.1.

	A	B	C	D	E	F
1	January	February	March	April	May	
2						
3						
4						

FIGURE 2.1: *Use AutoFill to extend a series when you select data that Excel recognizes as a sequence.*

To create an incremental series of numbers, enter the first two numbers of the series then select the range that contains the numbers and drag the range's fill handle. You must enter at least two numbers to tell Excel:

• What number to start the series with.

• How much to increment by.

To create an incremental series, follow these steps:

1. Enter **5** in cell A3 and **10** in cell A4.

2. Select A3:A4 and move the mouse pointer to the fill handle.

3. Drag down through cell A10. The numbers 15, 20, 25, 30, 35, and 40 appear in the cells, as shown in Figure 2.2.

	A	B
1	January	February
2		
3	5	
4	10	
5	15	
6	20	
7	25	
8	30	
9	35	
10	40	
11		

FIGURE 2.2: *Extending an incremental selection*

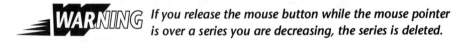 *You can fill a series of numbers with an automatic increment of 1. Select the cell that contains the number, then hold down Ctrl while you drag the fill handle through adjacent cells.*

Enter a series that *decreases* in value by dragging the fill handle up or to the left, as described here:

1. Suppose your series is 5, 10, 15, and you want to extend it to –15. Select the series.

2. Drag its fill handle up or to the left until the cells are filled. Notice as you drag through the series that each cell and its data appears in a crosshatched pattern.

3. Release the mouse button when all the cells you want to fill are highlighted.

If you release the mouse button while the mouse pointer is over a series you are decreasing, the series is deleted.

Copying Data with AutoFill

Use AutoFill to copy data into cells. For example, if you type **16** in cell B4 then select the cell and drag its fill handle through C4, D4, E4, and F4, 16 will appear in each cell when you release the mouse button.

ACTION *To copy data that Excel recognizes as the beginning of a series, such as* January *or* Monday, *hold down* **Ctrl** *while you drag the fill handle of the selected cell.*

Copy the data in a selected cell by double-clicking on its fill handle if cells in the adjacent column already contain data. For example, look at Figure 2.3. If A1:A10 contains data and you enter **$14.00** in B1 and then select the cell, you can double-click on its fill handle to fill cells B2:B10 with $14.00.

	A	B	C
1	Monday	$14.00	
2	Tuesday	$14.00	
3	Wednesday	$14.00	
4	Thursday	$14.00	
5	Friday	$14.00	
6	Saturday	$14.00	
7	Sunday	$14.00	
8	Monday	$14.00	
9	Tuesday	$14.00	
10	Wednesday	$14.00	
11			

FIGURE 2.3: *Copy data into cells in an adjacent column by double-clicking on the first cell's fill handle.*

Using the AutoFill Shortcut Menu

Use the AutoFill shortcut menu to create a series or copy data.

1. Enter the data you want to extend in the first cell, then select the cell.

2. Hold down the right mouse button while you drag the fill handle through the cells you want to copy data into or for which you want to enter a series.

3. Release the right mouse button. The AutoFill shortcut menu appears.

4. Select **Copy Cells** to copy the data into the cells or **Fill Series** to create a series with the value in the selected cell as the beginning of the series.

• • • **Saving a Workbook**

Save data you have entered to a file on your disk.

1. Click on the **Save** button on the Standard toolbar or choose File ➤ Save (**Ctrl+S**). If the file has not previously been saved, the Save As dialog box appears as shown in Figure 2.4.

2. By default, Excel saves all files as workbook files. Type the name you want for your file in the File Name text box. Excel will automatically add the .XLS file extension.

3. To change the directory where the workbook file will be stored, double-click on the name of directory in the Directories list box. The current path (where the file will be stored) appears just above the Directories list box.

4. Press ↵ or click **OK** to save the file.

Save a file often as you are working in it. Then, in case of a power outage or some other disaster, you won't have to reenter too much data.

Once a file has been saved, choose File ➤ Save As only if you want to rename the file.

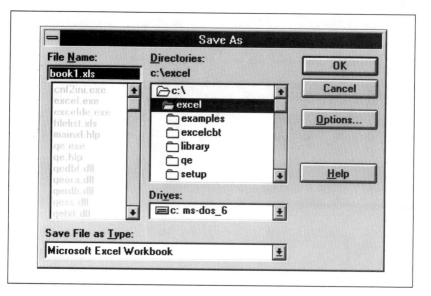

FIGURE 2.4: *The Save As dialog box appears the first time you save a new file.*

• • • Printing Your Data

Click on the **Print** button on the Standard toolbar or select File ➤ Print (**Ctrl+P**), then click **OK** or press ↵ to print the worksheet. Chapter 9 contains additional information about printing a worksheet.

 It's a good idea to save your data before you print it, just in case some type of system error occurs during the printing.

• • • Exiting Excel

When you are finished using Excel, always exit properly before you exit Windows. Excel asks you to save any files that you have changed since they were last saved, and removes any temporary files it created during your Excel session.

To exit Excel correctly:

- Double-click on Excel's Control menu icon or press **Alt+F4**.
- Press **Alt+Spacebar** or click on Excel's Control menu icon, then choose Close (**C**).
- Select File ➤ Exit.

Working with Formulas

● ● ● ● ● ● *fast track*

To tell Excel that data is a formula, type an = (equals sign) first.

To tell Excel to calculate part of a formula first, type parentheses around it.

To paste one of Excel's functions into a cell and then build its formula, use the Function Wizard.

ONE of the basic uses of a worksheet is to perform calculations on values. Excel calculates formulas entered into the cells of a worksheet.

... **Using Operators**

A formula must begin with an = (equals sign) so Excel can recognize that your data is a formula. You can use numbers, called *constants*, cell references, such as A6 or B3, or *range names* (meaningful names you assign to a worksheet range) as the values in your formulas. Use arithmetic or comparative *operators* to indicate what actions you want to perform with the values. You can use any of the operators in Table 3.1 in a formula.

OPERATOR	FUNCTION
+	addition
−	subtraction or negation
/	division
*	multiplication
%	percentage
^	exponentiation
= (equal)	comparison
> (greater than)	comparison
< (less than)	comparison
>= (greater than or equal to)	comparison
<= (less than or equal to)	comparison
<> (not equal to)	comparison

TABLE 3.1: *Excel's Arithmetic and Comparative Operators*

NOTE *The formula appears in both the cell and the formula bar as you type. Once you enter the formula, you can see the formula in the formula bar when you select the cell.*

By default, formulas are not displayed in a worksheet. If you type the formula **=4+6** in a cell and then press ↵, Excel calculates the value of the formula and displays its result, *10*, in the cell.

Use parentheses to indicate which set of values is calculated first in a more complex formula. If you enter the formula **=6+8*10** in a cell, Excel calculates the results as *86*, because multiplication takes precedence over addition. Excel performed the 8*10 calculation and then added 6 to it. However, if you enter **=(6+8)*10** in a cell, Excel calculates the operation in parentheses first (6+8=14) and multiplies 14 by 10 to give the result *140*.

Error Values

If you enter a formula that Excel cannot calculate, Excel will tell you by returning an *error value*. Error values begin with a # (number sign) followed by specific text. You must edit the formula so Excel can correctly calculate its results.

• • • Editing a Formula

Select the cell that contains the formula you want to change, then click in the entry area of the formula bar to place the insertion point where you want to change the data. Or press **F2** (the Edit key) to place the insertion point at the end of the data in the cell.

Use any of the following editing methods:

- Move the insertion point by either clicking in a different location or by pressing the ← and → keys.
- When the insertion point is where you want to add data, type the new data.
- To delete the character to the right of the insertion point, press **Del**.
- To delete the character to the left of the insertion point, press **Backspace**.

- Drag to highlight any characters you want to replace, then type the new characters.

- Press ↵ or click the enter box on the formula bar to enter the edited data.

··· Using Worksheet Functions

Excel comes with some formulas, called *functions*, already built-in. Use Excel's worksheet functions to help you create and simplify formulas.

1. Type = (equals sign) if the function is the beginning of the formula, then type the function's name followed by the left parenthesis.

2. Type the function's *arguments*, the values on which you want to perform operations.

3. Type the right parenthesis to close the formula.

4. Press ↵ to enter the formula and display its results.

The Sum Function

Use Excel's SUM function to add the values in a range of cells or in non-adjacent cells.

Suppose you enter **10** in A1, **20** in A2, and **30** in A3. Select A5 and type **=SUM(A1:A3)**, then press ↵ to show that *60* is the total.

 Excel's functions are not case-sensitive. You can use either uppercase or lowercase letters in the function's name.

Using AutoSum

There is an even easier way to calculate the sum of the values in cells A1, A2, and A3 in the above example, and that is to use Excel's *AutoSum* feature. Follow these steps:

1. Select cell A5 then click on the **AutoSum** button on the Standard toolbar. AutoSum automatically suggests that all the cells above it (A1, A2, A3, and A4, even though the latter is empty), be included in the formula.

2. Press ↵ to enter the formula into the cell.

3. Now select cell C7 and click on the **AutoSum** button. No cells are suggested because there are no values in column C or row 7.

4. To select the values to total, drag through cells A1, A2, and A3.

5. Click on the enter box on the formula bar to enter the SUM function into the cell.

Use AutoSum to simultaneously enter more than one sum:

1. Select the row where you want the sums of values in corresponding columns to appear, as shown in Figure 3.1.

2. Click the **AutoSum** button.

To total the values in rows, select the column where you want the totals to appear and click the **AutoSum** button, as shown in Figure 3.2.

	A	B	C	D	E	F	G
1		January	February	March	April	Qtr. 1 Total	
2							
3	Rent	$1,200.00	$1,200.00	$1,200.00	$1,200.00		
4	Insurance	$325.00	$325.00	$325.00	$325.00		
5	Telephone	$130.00	$130.00	$130.00	$130.00		
6	Postage	$100.00	$100.00	$100.00	$100.00		
7							
8	TOTAL	$1,755.00	$1,755.00	$1,755.00	$1,755.00		
9							

FIGURE 3.1: *Use AutoSum to total columns of data simultaneously.*

	A	B	C	D	E	F	G
1		January	February	March	April	Qtr. 1 Total	
2							
3	Rent	$1,200.00	$1,200.00	$1,200.00	$1,200.00	$4,800.00	
4	Insurance	$325.00	$325.00	$325.00	$325.00	$1,300.00	
5	Telephone	$130.00	$130.00	$130.00	$130.00	$520.00	
6	Postage	$100.00	$100.00	$100.00	$100.00	$400.00	
7						$0.00	
8	TOTAL	$1,755.00	$1,755.00	$1,755.00	$1,755.00	$7,020.00	
9							

FIGURE 3.2: *Totaling rows of data with AutoSum*

Use AutoSum to simultaneously total the values in both rows and columns. Select the rows and columns you want to total and also the cells where you want the totals to appear, as shown in Figure 3.3. Then click the **AutoSum** button.

	A	B	C	D	E	F	G
1		January	February	March	April	Qtr. 1 Total	
2							
3	Rent	$1,200.00	$1,200.00	$1,200.00	$1,200.00	$4,800.00	
4	Insurance	$325.00	$325.00	$325.00	$325.00	$1,300.00	
5	Telephone	$130.00	$130.00	$130.00	$130.00	$520.00	
6	Postage	$100.00	$100.00	$100.00	$100.00	$400.00	
7							
8	TOTAL	$1,755.00	$1,755.00	$1,755.00	$1,755.00	$7,020.00	
9							

FIGURE 3.3: *Select the data and the cells where you want the totals to appear to total both rows and columns.*

If your worksheet includes subtotaled rows or columns of data, use AutoSum to calculate the grand totals:

1. Select all the data, including the constant values in the worksheet and select the row or column where you want the grand totals to appear, as shown in Figure 3.4.

	A	B	C	D	E	F	G
1		January	February	March	April	Qtr. 1 Total	
2							
3	Rent	$1,200.00	$1,200.00	$1,200.00	$1,200.00	$4,800.00	
4	Insurance	$325.00	$325.00	$325.00	$325.00	$1,300.00	
5	Telephone	$130.00	$130.00	$130.00	$130.00	$520.00	
6	Postage	$100.00	$100.00	$100.00	$100.00	$400.00	
7							
8	TOTAL	$1,755.00	$1,755.00	$1,755.00	$1,755.00	$7,020.00	
9							
10	Office Supplies	$500.00	$500.00	$500.00	$500.00	$2,000.00	
11	Furniture	$600.00	$600.00	$600.00	$600.00	$2,400.00	
12	Equipment	$1,400.00	$1,400.00	$1,400.00	$1,400.00	$5,600.00	
13							
14	TOTAL	$2,500.00	$2,500.00	$2,500.00	$2,500.00	$10,000.00	
15	GRAND TOTAL	$4,255.00	$4,255.00	$4,255.00	$4,255.00	$17,020.00	
16							

FIGURE 3.4: *Use AutoSum to calculate grand totals.*

2. Click the **AutoSum** button. AutoSum ignores the constants in your worksheet and calculates the values in the cells that contain formulas.

• • • Using the Function Wizard

Use the *Function Wizard* to easily access any of Excel's functions and correctly build its arguments in a formula.

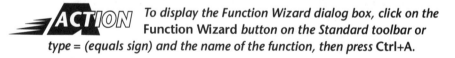 *To display the Function Wizard dialog box, click on the* Function Wizard *button on the Standard toolbar or type = (equals sign) and the name of the function, then press* **Ctrl+A.**

1. Select the cell where you want to place a formula.

2. Type = (equals sign) to activate the formula bar.

3. Click on the **Function Wizard** button. The Function Wizard - Step 1 of 2 dialog box appears, similar to Figure 3.5.

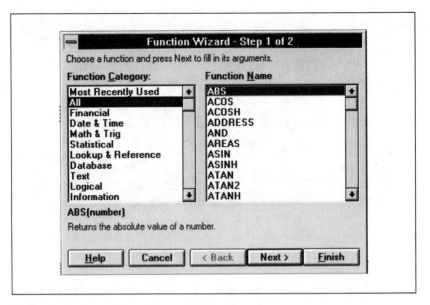

FIGURE 3.5: *The Function Wizard dialog box*

4. Press **S** to scroll through the **Function Name** list box to the first function that begins with an *S*. Then press ↓ until SUM is highlighted in the list box.

5. Click on Next or press ↵ to start building the formula. The Function Wizard - Step 2 of 2 dialog box appears.

6. Type each number you want to total (or the cell reference of each value), followed by a comma, in the **number 1** text box. Do not type any spaces in the formula.

7. Press ↵ or click on Finish.

8. Press ↵ to enter the formula in the cell.

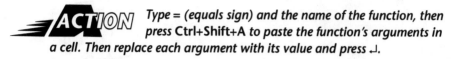 *Type = (equals sign) and the name of the function, then press* **Ctrl+Shift+A** *to paste the function's arguments in a cell. Then replace each argument with its value and press ↲.*

To edit a formula that contains a function, select the cell that contains the formula and click in the formula bar, then click on the **Function Wizard** button.

4

Editing Your Data

To display the Open dialog box, click on the **Open** button on the Standard toolbar.

To move or copy selected data, click on the **Cut** or **Copy** button on the Standard toolbar.

To paste the contents of the Clipboard in a selected cell or range, click on the **Paste** button on the Standard toolbar.

FREQUENTLY worksheet data needs to be edited. In this chapter, you will see how to open a workbook file, move and copy data, and reverse your last action. You are guided through inserting and deleting cells, columns, and rows in a worksheet.

・・・ **Opening a Workbook File**

Excel's files are saved as workbooks by default. Once you have saved a workbook to a file on a disk, you can open the workbook file to edit it.

 The last four files you have opened appear on the File menu. Select a file's name to open it.

To open a file, choose File ➤ Open (**Ctrl+O**). The Open dialog box appears, similar to Figure 4.1

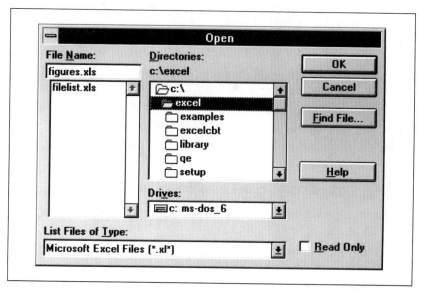

FIGURE 4.1: *The Open dialog box allows you to open a file in a different drive or directory.*

 Click on the Open button on the Standard toolbar to display the Open dialog box.

1. Double-click on the subdirectory where the file is stored in the Directories list box.

2. Double-click on the name of the file you want to open in the File Name list box.

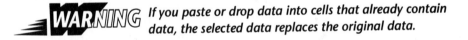

Hold down **Ctrl** *while you click on additional file names in the File Name list box, then click* **OK** *to simultaneously open more than one workbook file.*

··· Moving and Copying Worksheet Data

To rearrange the data in a worksheet, move or copy data to different locations. Moved data is removed from its current location and placed somewhere else. Copied data is placed in a different location while keeping the original in the same place.

There are two ways to move or copy data. You can cut or copy data to the Windows clipboard and paste it in a different location, or you can move or copy data with *drag-and-drop*.

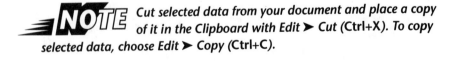

If you paste or drop data into cells that already contain data, the selected data replaces the original data.

Using Cut, Copy, and Paste

To cut or copy and then paste information, follow these steps:

1. Select the data you want to move or copy.

2. Click the **Cut** button on the Standard toolbar to move the data or the **Copy** button to copy the data. Or click the right mouse button on the selection and choose Cut or Copy.

Cut selected data from your document and place a copy of it in the Clipboard with Edit ➤ *Cut (Ctrl+X). To copy selected data, choose Edit* ➤ *Copy (Ctrl+C).*

3. Select the cell where you want to place a copy of the data that is in the Clipboard and click the **Paste** button on the Standard toolbar. Or right-click on the cell and click on Paste.

NOTE *Select the top-left cell of the range in the worksheet where you want to paste a range of data. A range is pasted down and to the right.*

You can paste the data in the Clipboard into Excel or another Windows application as many times as you like. It remains in the Clipboard until you cut or copy other data.

Using Drag-and-Drop

Use your mouse to "drag" data you want to move or copy and "drop" it in another location. You can use drag-and-drop only within the area that is displayed on your screen.

To move data, follow these steps:

1. Select the data.

2. Point to the border of the cell or range.

3. When the mouse pointer appears as an arrow, drag the selection to a different location. As you drag, a cross-hatched border appears where the data will be placed.

4. When the border appears in the location you want, release the mouse button to drop the data.

To copy cells by dragging, follow the steps above, but hold down **Ctrl** while you drag the data to a different location.

 You can also use the AutoFill handle to copy selected data to adjacent cells.

• • • Deleting Data

There are several ways to delete selected worksheet data.

- Press the **Del** key.
- Right-click on the selection to display the shortcut menu and select Clear Contents.
- Select Edit ➤ Clear, then choose Contents.

• • • Undoing a Command or Action

You can undo many (but not all) commands or actions in Excel. If a command or action cannot be undone, the Undo command becomes Can't Undo.

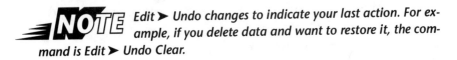 Edit ➤ Undo changes to indicate your last action. For example, if you delete data and want to restore it, the command is Edit ➤ Undo Clear.

To undo your last action:

- Click on the **Undo** button on the Standard toolbar.
- Select Edit ➤ Undo.
- Press **Ctrl+Z**.

 To undo the undo, immediately click on the Redo button on the Standard toolbar, select Edit ➤ Redo, or press Ctrl+Z.

• • • Inserting a Cell, Row, or Column

There are several ways to insert a cell, row, or column in a sheet:

1. Select the cell or cells where you want to insert new, blank cells.

2. Choose Insert ➤ Cells to display the Insert dialog box, as shown in Figure 4.2.

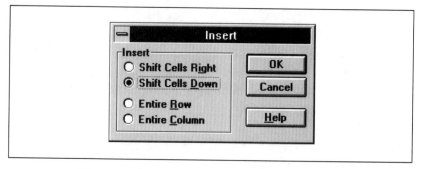

FIGURE 4.2: *The Insert dialog box appears when you select a cell and choose Insert ➤ Cells.*

3. Select **Shift Cells Right** to move all the data in the row, beginning with the selection, to the right and insert blank cells. Or choose **Shift Cells Down** to move all the data in the column, starting with the selection, down, and insert blank cells.

4. Press ↵ or click **OK** in the Insert dialog box.

NOTE *You can choose Entire Row or Entire Column in the Insert dialog box to insert a blank row or column in the position of a selected cell.*

To insert a row or column:

• Select a cell or cells in the rows or the row headings, then choose Insert ➤ Rows.

• Select a cell or cells in the columns or the column headings, then choose Insert ➤ Columns.

• • • Deleting a Cell, Row, or Column

To delete a cell, follow these steps:

1. Select the cell(s) you want to delete.

2. Choose Edit ➤ Delete. The Delete dialog box appears, as shown in Figure 4.3.

3. Choose **Shift Cells Left** to remove the cells and replace them with the cells in the same row to the right of the selection. Or choose **Shift Cells Up** to remove the cells and replace them with the cells in the column below the selection.

4. Press ↵ or click **OK** in the Delete dialog box.

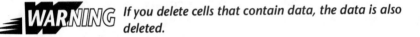 *If you delete cells that contain data, the data is also deleted.*

To delete a row or column:

- Select a cell or cells where you want to delete rows, choose Edit ➤ Delete, then choose Entire Row and click **OK**.

- Select the headings of the rows you want to delete and choose Edit ➤ Delete.

- Select a cell or cells where you want to delete columns, choose Edit ➤ Delete, then choose Entire Column and click **OK**.

- Select the headings of the columns you want to delete and choose Edit ➤ Delete.

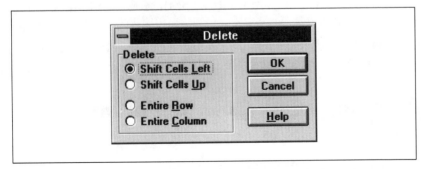

FIGURE 4.3: *The Delete dialog box appears when you select a cell then choose Edit ➤ Delete.*

Using Workbooks

5

As you know, Excel's files are groups of worksheets called *workbooks*. Each new workbook you open contains 16 worksheets by default.

... Moving between Sheets

After you enter data on the first worksheet, you may want to select a different worksheet to enter related data.

To select the tab of the worksheet you want to activate:

- Click on the tab of the worksheet.
- Hold down **Ctrl** while you click on several worksheet tabs.
- Press **Ctrl+Page Down** to select the next sheet.
- Press **Ctrl+Page Up** to select the previous sheet.

To select a sheet with your mouse, that sheet's tab must appear on your screen. Originally, six tabs appear on your screen as shown in Figure 5.1.

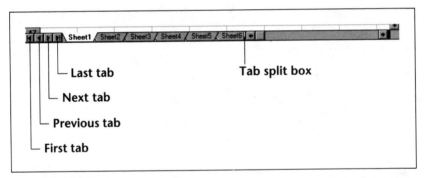

FIGURE 5.1: *The worksheet tabs and scrolling buttons that appear when you first open a new workbook.*

Use the tab scroll buttons to display other worksheet tabs in the workbook.

- Click on the **first tab** or **last tab** scroll button to display the first or last tab in the workbook.
- Click on the **next tab** or **previous tab** button to display the next or previous tab in the workbook.

 *If the tab does not appear on your screen, drag the tab split box to the right to display more tabs. Double-click on the tab split box to reset the scroll bar to its original size.*

... Adding a Sheet to a Workbook

Select the tab of the sheet where you want to add a new, blank, worksheet. Then select Insert ➤ Worksheet (**Shift+F11**) to insert a new worksheet in front of the active worksheet, as shown in Figure 5.2.

FIGURE 5.2: *Inserting a new worksheet in a workbook*

... Deleting a Worksheet

Select the tab of a worksheet you want to delete, then choose Edit ➤ Delete Sheet. Choose **OK** to confirm that you want to permanently delete the selected sheet.

 *If you select several sheets at once and then choose Edit ➤ Delete Sheet, all the selected sheets will be deleted.*

... Renaming Worksheets

The worksheets in a workbook are originally named Sheet 1, Sheet 2, etc.

1. Select the tab of the sheet you want to rename.

2. Choose Format ➤ Sheet ➤ Rename.

3. Type the name for the sheet in the Name text box.

4. Select **OK** in the Rename Sheet dialog box.

The name you assign to a worksheet can contain up to 31 characters and can include spaces.

• • • **Rearranging Sheets within a Workbook**

Select the sheet you want to move, then drag its tab to a different location. A small downward-pointing black triangle appears. When the triangle is pointing to the location where you want the sheet, release the mouse button. Figure 5.3 shows Sheet 1 moved in front of Sheet 5.

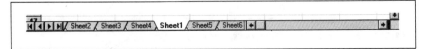

FIGURE 5.3: *Sheet 1 is moved in front of Sheet 5.*

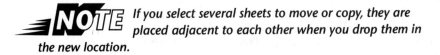 *If you select several sheets to move or copy, they are placed adjacent to each other when you drop them in the new location.*

Select the sheet you want to copy, then hold down **Ctrl** while you drag its tab to a different location. When the triangle is pointing to the location where you want the copy, release the mouse button. Excel renames the copy of the sheet with the same name as the original and *(2)*, as shown in Figure 5.4.

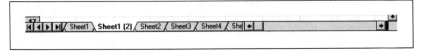

FIGURE 5.4: *Excel renames the sheet you copy.*

··· Moving and Copying Sheets to a Different Workbook

To move or copy a worksheet to a new or open workbook, follow these steps:

1. Select the sheet you want to move or copy.

2. Select Edit ➤ Move or Copy Sheet to display the Move or Copy dialog box shown in Figure 5.5.

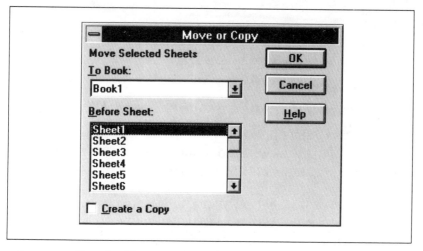

FIGURE 5.5: *Use the Move or Copy dialog box to place a sheet in a different workbook.*

TIP *If you have both workbooks displayed on your screen, you can drag a worksheet to move it or press the **Ctrl** key while you drag to copy it to a different workbook.*

3. Click on the To Book drop-down list, then select (new book) or the name of the workbook where you want to place the worksheet or a copy.

4. If you selected a workbook name in step 3, click on the name of the sheet whose tab you want to the right of the worksheet you are moving or copying in the Before Sheet list box.

5. If you are copying the worksheet, select the Create a Copy check box.

6. Select **OK** in the Move or Copy dialog box.

· · · Using Workbook Windows

To compare different parts of a worksheet, different sheets in a workbook, or different sheets in different workbooks, you can arrange open windows on your screen.

Opening and Arranging Worksheet Windows

To display two different views of a worksheet, or two different worksheets in the same workbook simultaneously, open the workbook that contains the worksheets.

1. Choose Window ➤ New Window. A window with the same name (but with a *2* beside the name on the title bar) appears.

2. Select Window ➤ Arrange to display the Arrange Windows dialog box, shown in Figure 5.6.

3. To display only the open windows of the active workbook if other workbook windows are open, select the Windows of Active Workbook check box.

4. Select **OK** in the Arrange Windows dialog box.

Any changes you make in one open window of a workbook are also reflected in the other open windows of the same workbook, because, after all, the two windows are really just showing different sections of the same workbook. Save the workbook file to save your changes.

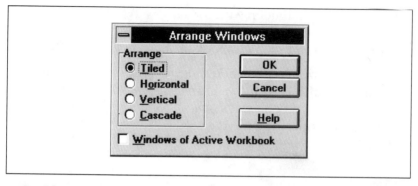

FIGURE 5.6: *The Arrange Windows dialog box lets you arrange the open windows of the active workbook or all open windows.*

 To display a different worksheet in one of the open windows, just click on its tab as you would normally.

You can activate only one open window at a time. To make a window active, do either of the following:

- If multiple windows are arranged on your screen, click anywhere in the window you want to activate.

- Choose Window ➤ *N* to activate the window you want on the numbered list.

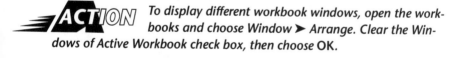 To display different workbook windows, open the workbooks and choose Window ➤ Arrange. Clear the Windows of Active Workbook check box, then choose OK.

Working with Open Windows

You can manipulate open windows to meet your needs.

- To hide the active window without closing it, choose Window ➤ Hide.

- To redisplay a hidden window, choose Window ➤ Unhide, then click on the name of the window you want to display in the Unhide Workbook list box and choose **OK**.

- To close a workbook window, double-click on its control icon. If multiple windows in the same workbook are open, the workbook stays open. If only one workbook window is open, the file is closed.

Cell References and Names

• • • • • • fast track

To define a name in a worksheet, use Insert ➤ Name ➤ Define.

To let Excel create names based on titles entered in columns or rows, use Insert ➤ Name ➤ Create.

IN this chapter, you will learn how to move or copy formulas with absolute and relative references. You will learn how to name a cell or a range, and how to use range operators to select data.

... **Cell References**

Each cell or range in a worksheet has a specific name, called a *reference*. The original name of a cell or range is also its location. For example, C4 is the cell in row 4 of column C, and D6:E8 is the group of adjacent cells that begins with D6 and ends with E8.

≡ACTION *After you type an operator, click on the cell or drag through the range you want to include in a formula, then click on the enter box or press ↵ to enter the formula.*

Use cell or range references in formulas to indicate the values in the cells. There are several kinds of references you can use in your formulas.

Relative References

Relative references tell Excel where to find a value in a worksheet. Use a relative reference to find another cell beginning with (relative to) the cell that contains the formula. A relative reference tells Excel to "go down three rows and over two columns" to find the value. Relative references are the default, and are designated *C4* or *G9*.

Absolute References

An *absolute* reference tells Excel the exact location of a cell, like saying "always use the value in C4." You must tell Excel when to use an absolute reference by adding a $ (dollar sign) in front of the column letter and row number. For example, *$C$4* is the absolute reference of the value in C4.

Mixed References

Combine relative and absolute references in Excel to form *mixed* references. Add the $ before either the row or column, whichever is to be absolute.

· · · Moving and Copying References and Formulas

Moving and copying data or a formula can affect how the formula is calculated.

In Figure 6.1, the formula in cell A7 is

=SUM(A1:A2)-1

If you move the value in A2 (which is *20*) to E1, the formula in A7 stays the same, but its result is changed to *9*.

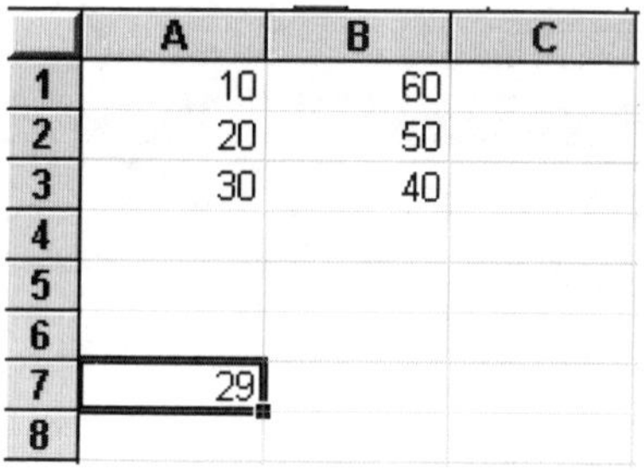

	A	B	C
1	10	60	
2	20	50	
3	30	40	
4			
5			
6			
7	29		
8			

FIGURE 6.1: *Moving data affects the results of a calculation.*

If you copy the formula in A7 to B7, the formula in B7 becomes

=SUM(B1:B2)-1

and the result is *109*. The *relative* references of A1:A2 were copied to the formula in B7. However, if you change the formula in A7 to include the absolute references of the range

=SUM($A$1:$A$2)–1

then copy the formula to B7, the *absolute* references are copied to the formula in B7 and the result is *9*.

• • • **Cell or Range Names**

You can assign meaningful names to cells or ranges in a worksheet. The names can be used in formulas and dialog boxes, or anywhere cell or range references are used.

1. Select the cell or range you want to name.

2. Choose Insert ➤ Name ➤ Define. The Define Name dialog box appears, similar to Figure 6.2.

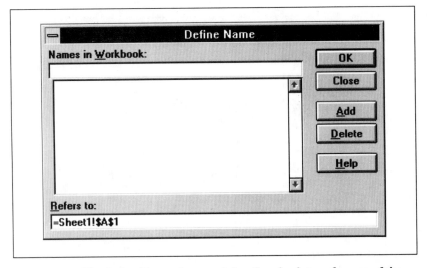

FIGURE 6.2: *The Refers To text box contains the absolute reference of the cells you selected.*

3. Type the name you want for the selection in the Names in Workbook text box. The Refers To text box displays the name of the worksheet and the absolute reference of the cell or range you selected.

4. Click **OK** or press ↵ to define the name in the workbook.

NOTE *The name of the worksheet is displayed in the name reference as* **Sheet1!** *Names you assign to a worksheet are used throughout the workbook. To use the same name on a different sheet, type the name of the sheet, followed by an exclamation mark, then the range in the Names in Workbook text box. Then select* **OK**.

Excel can create names for cells or ranges based on titles you entered for columns and rows. Look at the worksheet in Figure 6.3. Excel can create names using text in row 1 as the name of each column and text in column A as the name of each row.

	A	B	C	D	E	F	G
1		January	February	March	April	Qtr. 1 Total	
2							
3	Rent	$1,200.00	$1,200.00	$1,200.00	$1,200.00	$4,800.00	
4	Insurance	$325.00	$325.00	$325.00	$325.00	$1,300.00	
5	Telephone	$130.00	$130.00	$130.00	$130.00	$520.00	
6	Postage	$100.00	$100.00	$100.00	$100.00	$400.00	
7						$0.00	
8	TOTAL	$1,755.00	$1,755.00	$1,755.00	$1,755.00	$7,020.00	
9							

FIGURE 6.3: *Have Excel create names for ranges based on titles you entered in the worksheet.*

1. Select both the names and the cells you want to name. In Figure 6.3 for example, drag through A1:F8.

2. Choose Insert ➤ Name ➤ Create. The Create Names dialog box appears, as shown in Figure 6.4.

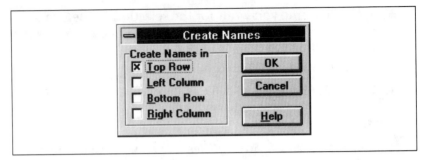

FIGURE 6.4: *The Create Names dialog box lets you choose which names Excel will create.*

3. Select the check box for each set of range names you want Excel to create. For the data in Figure 6.2 you could select the Top Row (which is already selected) and Left Column check boxes.

4. Select **OK**.

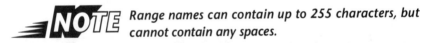 *Range names can contain up to 255 characters, but cannot contain any spaces.*

To see the names that are defined or created in a workbook, select Insert ➤ Name ➤ Define to display the Define Name dialog box.

*To delete a name from the workbook, display the Define Names dialog box, select the name you want to delete in the Names in Workbook list box, then select **Delete** and choose **OK** in the Define Names dialog box.*

To select a named range, click the Name drop-down list button on the formula bar, then click on the name of the range you want to select. Figure 6.5 shows the range named *January* selected in the worksheet.

	A	B	C	D	E	F	G
1		January	February	March	April	Qtr. 1 Total	
2							
3	Rent	$1,200.00	$1,200.00	$1,200.00	$1,200.00	$4,800.00	
4	Insurance	$325.00	$325.00	$325.00	$325.00	$1,300.00	
5	Telephone	$130.00	$130.00	$130.00	$130.00	$520.00	
6	Postage	$100.00	$100.00	$100.00	$100.00	$400.00	
7						$0.00	
8	TOTAL	$1,755.00	$1,755.00	$1,755.00	$1,755.00	$7,020.00	
9							

FIGURE 6.5: *Type "January" in the Name box on the formula bar, then press ↵ to select the range.*

• • • Reference Operators

Just as there are operators to define the action you want to perform in a formula, there are three operators to define how to use references in a formula.

> **Range**, represented by a colon, indicates one reference to all the cells in the range. A range appears as *A3:B6*.

> **Union**, represented by a comma, indicates a reference combined from multiple references. A union appears as *A3:F3,E1:E8* or *Rent,April*, as shown in Figure 6.6.

	A	B	C	D	E	F	G
1		January	February	March	April	Qtr. 1 Total	
2							
3	Rent	$1,200.00	$1,200.00	$1,200.00	$1,200.00	$4,800.00	
4	Insurance	$325.00	$325.00	$325.00	$325.00	$1,300.00	
5	Telephone	$130.00	$130.00	$130.00	$130.00	$520.00	
6	Postage	$100.00	$100.00	$100.00	$100.00	$400.00	
7						$0.00	
8	TOTAL	$1,755.00	$1,755.00	$1,755.00	$1,755.00	$7,020.00	
9							

FIGURE 6.6: *The union of Rent and April*

Intersection, represented by a space, indicates a common reference within multiple references. An intersection appears as *A3:F3 E1:E8* or *Rent April*, as shown in Figure 6.7.

	A	B	C	D	E	F	G
1		January	February	March	April	Qtr. 1 Total	
2							
3	Rent	$1,200.00	$1,200.00	$1,200.00	$1,200.00	$4,800.00	
4	Insurance	$325.00	$325.00	$325.00	$325.00	$1,300.00	
5	Telephone	$130.00	$130.00	$130.00	$130.00	$520.00	
6	Postage	$100.00	$100.00	$100.00	$100.00	$400.00	
7						$0.00	
8	TOTAL	$1,755.00	$1,755.00	$1,755.00	$1,755.00	$7,020.00	
9							

FIGURE 6.7: *The intersection of Rent and April*

Formatting a Worksheet

• • • • • • *fast track*

To change the width of a column, drag the right column heading border.

To change the height of a row, drag the bottom row heading border.

To apply borders to selected cells, use the **Borders** button on the Formatting toolbar.

To apply a built-in format to your data, select Format ➤ AutoFormat.

ENHANCE the appearance of your worksheet by changing its format. In this chapter, you will see how to change the height of a row, the width of a column, hide a row or column of data, and hide an entire worksheet in a workbook.

··· **Changing the Row Height or Column Width**

To include data in a worksheet that requires a higher row or a wider column than appears in the original worksheet grid, change the row height and column width with your mouse.

> **TIP** *While you drag the border of a row to change its height or of a column to change its width, the current measurement of the row or column appears in the Name box on the formula bar.*

To change the height of a row or the width of a column, move the mouse pointer on the heading's lower or right border. When the mouse pointer changes into a bar intersected by a two-headed arrow, drag the border to change the height or width, as shown in Figure 7.1.

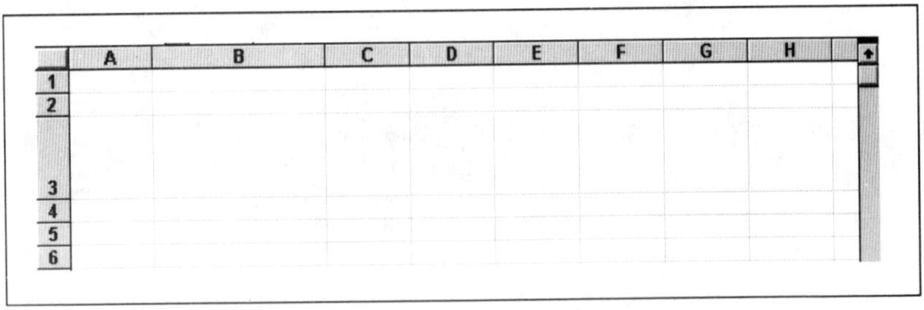

FIGURE 7.1: *Increasing the height of row 3 and the width of column B*

There are several other ways to change the row height and column width:

- Select a cell in the row you want to change, then choose Format ➤ Row ➤ Height. Type the number of points for the height of the row in the Row Height text box, then choose **OK** to change the height of the entire row.

- Select a cell in the column whose width you want to change, then choose Format ➤ Column ➤ Width. Type the width (in characters) in the Column Width text box and choose **OK**.

- Select a row or several rows and choose Format ➤ Row ➤ AutoFit. The row height for each selected row is assigned according to the font size of the row.

- Double-click on the bottom border of the row heading to automatically adjust the height of the row according to the font size.

- Select a column, then choose Format ➤ Column ➤ AutoFit Selection to adjust the column to the smallest width necessary to display its contents.

- Double-click on the column heading's right border to automatically adjust the column to its minimum width.

- To reset the column to its default width, select a cell in the column, then choose Format ➤ Column ➤ Standard Width and choose **OK**.

- To change the width of all columns in the worksheet not previously changed, select a cell in an unchanged column, and choose Format ➤ Column ➤ Standard Width, type the number of characters the columns will hold in the Standard Column Width text box, and choose **OK**.

Hiding a Row or Column

When you hide a row or column of data in a worksheet, the display of the entire row or column is hidden, as shown in Figure 7.2. The column letter and row number are missing, and the border is wider between displayed columns and rows to indicate that a column or row is hidden.

 *The data in a hidden row or column will not print when you print the worksheet.*

	A	B	C	D	F	G
1		January	February	March	Qtr. 1 Total	
2						
3	Rent	$1,200.00	$1,200.00	$1,200.00	$4,800.00	
4	Insurance	$325.00	$325.00	$325.00	$1,300.00	
5	Telephone	$130.00	$130.00	$130.00	$520.00	
6	Postage	$100.00	$100.00	$100.00	$400.00	
8	TOTAL	$1,755.00	$1,755.00	$1,755.00	$7,020.00	
9						

FIGURE 7.2: *Column E and row 7 are hidden.*

To hide a column of data, select a cell in the column or click on the column heading to select the whole column. Then choose Format ➤ Column ➤ Hide (**Ctrl+0**).

ACTION *Use your mouse to hide a column or row. Drag the right border of a column heading until it meets the left column border or drag the bottom border of a row heading until it meets the top row border. Release the mouse button to hide the column or row.*

To hide a row of data, select a cell in the row or click on the row heading to select the entire row. Then choose Format ➤ Row ➤ Hide (**Ctrl+9**).

To redisplay a hidden column or row:

- Select the rows or columns on both sides of the hidden data, then choose Format ➤ Column ➤ Unhide (**Ctrl+Shift+)**) to redisplay a hidden column or Format ➤ Row ➤ Unhide (**Ctrl+Shift+(**) to redisplay a hidden row.

- Move the mouse pointer just to the right of the border that indicates a hidden column or just below the border that indicates a hidden row. When the mouse pointer changes into a double line with a two-headed arrow, drag the border to redisplay the column or row.

Hiding a Worksheet

Select the tab of the worksheet you want to hide, then choose Format ➤ Sheet ➤ Hide. There is no indication on your screen that a worksheet exists when it is hidden.

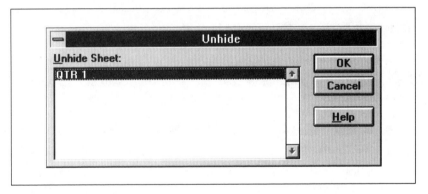

To tell if a worksheet is hidden in the active workbook, glance at the Format ➤ Sheet submenu. The Unhide command is only available if a worksheet is hidden.

To redisplay a hidden worksheet, select Format ➤ Sheet ➤ Unhide. The Unhide dialog box appears, similar to Figure 7.3. Highlight the name of the worksheet in the Unhide Sheet list box, then click **OK** or press ↵.

FIGURE 7.3: *Display the Unhide dialog box to select the worksheet you want to redisplay.*

••• Adding Borders and Shading

Add borders and shading to selected cells to enhance the appearance of a worksheet.

1. Select the cells then choose Format ➤ Cells (**Ctrl+1**).

2. Click on the **Border** tab, shown in Figure 7.4.

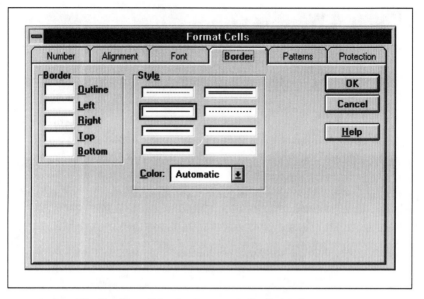

FIGURE 7.4: *The Border tab in the Format Cells dialog box*

 *Click on the* **Borders** *drop-down button on the Formatting toolbar to display your choices for adding a border to selected cells.*

3. Click on the description of the border you want for your selection.

4. Click on the style of line you want for the border in the Style area.

5. To add a pattern, click on the Patterns tab.

6. Click on the Pattern drop-down list button, then click on the pattern you want to use as shading.

7. Select **OK** in the Format Cells dialog box.

 *The* **Pattern** *button appears on the Drawing toolbar. See Chapter 12 for information about displaying another toolbar.*

••• Applying an AutoFormat

Excel comes with several built-in formats you can use to automatically format a worksheet. Use the AutoFormat feature to add borders and shading to cells in your worksheet.

1. Select the data or a cell in the range you want to automatically format.

2. Select Format ➤ AutoFormat to display the AutoFormat dialog box, shown in Figure 7.5.

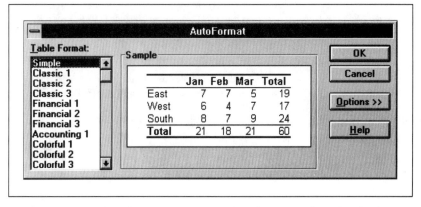

FIGURE 7.5: *Display the AutoFormat dialog box to select the built-in format for your data.*

3. Click on the name of the format in the Table Format list box.

4. Select **OK** to apply the format to your selection.

8

Formatting Your Data

•••••• *fast track*

To change the format of selected cells to currency with two decimal places, click on the **Currency Style** button on the Formatting toolbar.

To align data in selected cells, click on one of the alignment buttons on the Formatting toolbar.

To copy the format from a selected cell to other cells, click on the **Format Painter** button on the Standard toolbar.

CHANGE the format of your data from Excel's defaults to enhance the appearance of a worksheet. Use the Formatting toolbar or commands on the Format menu to change the appearance of data.

• • • Number Formats

Numbers are assigned the General number format by default in Excel. General number format shows the numbers exactly as you enter them in the worksheet. For example, if you enter **3.14159**, that number will appear in the cell.

NOTE *The format that you select for a number determines what you see in the cell, but Excel stores and calculates the number with up to fifteen decimal places.*

You can change the number format of selected cells. Suppose you want to make some cells in a worksheet appear as currency with dollar signs and two decimal places.

ACTION *Click on the* **Currency Style** *button on the Formatting toolbar to change the format of selected cells to currency with two decimal places.*

1. Select the cells in which you want to enter dollar amounts.
2. Choose Format ➤ Cells (**Ctrl+1**).
3. If necessary, click on the Number tab to display the Format Cells dialog box shown in Figure 8.1.
4. Select Currency in the Category list box.
5. Select the third entry in the Format Codes list box.
6. Click **OK** or press ↵.

• • • Changing the Font

You can change the font, font size, and attributes of characters in selected cells.

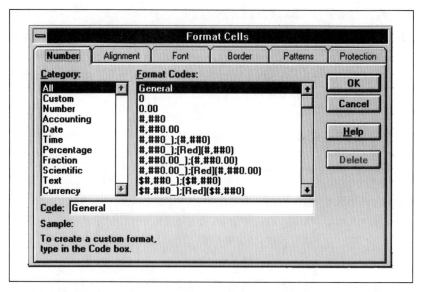

FIGURE 8.1: *The Number tab in the Format Cells dialog box*

TIP *The Formatting toolbar contains a variety of buttons to use as shortcuts for formatting data in the worksheet. For example, choose a font name in the Font drop-down list, and a size for the font in the Font Size drop-down list. You can click the **Bold** or **Italic** button to apply either style to the selected cells.*

1. Choose Format ➤ Cells (**Ctrl+1**).

2. Click on the Font tab, shown in Figure 8.2.

3. Select the name of the font in the Font list box.

4. Select the style of the font in the Font Style list box.

5. Select the size for the font in the Size list box.

6. Select **OK** in the Format Cells dialog box.

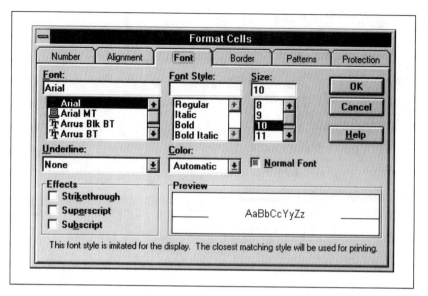

FIGURE 8.2: *The Font tab in the Format Cells dialog box*

ACTION Click on the Underline *button on the Formatting toolbar to place a single underline below the characters in* selected cells. Click on the Font Color *drop-down list, then click on the color in the palette for the characters in selected cells.*

There are some other options you can choose on the Font tab.

- To *underline* the characters in each selected cell, select the Underline drop-down list button, then select the type of underline you want in the list.

- To change the *color* of the characters in each selected cell, choose a color in the Color drop-down list.

- To place a *line* through the characters or make the characters *superscript* (place the characters in a smaller font higher on the line) or *subscript* (place the characters in a smaller font lower on the line), select the Strikethrough, Superscript, or Subscript check boxes.

··· Aligning Data in a Cell

Excel automatically aligns data in worksheet cells in *General* format (numbers are aligned along the right edge of cells and text is aligned along the left edge). Use buttons on the Formatting toolbar to change the alignment:

- Click on the **Align Left** button to align data along the left edge of selected cells.

- Click on the **Center** button to center data within selected cells.

- Click on the **Align Right** button to align data along the right edge of selected cells.

- Click on the **Center Across Columns** button to align the data in a cell over several selected cells in a row, as shown in Figure 8.3.

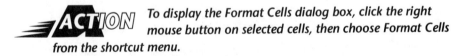

FIGURE 8.3: *Aligning data across cells in several columns*

ACTION — To display the Format Cells dialog box, click the right mouse button on selected cells, then choose Format Cells from the shortcut menu.

You can also change the alignment of data in selected cells with the Format Cells dialog box.

1. Select the cells whose alignment you want to change.

2. Choose Format ➤ Cells (**Ctrl+1**).

3. Click on the Alignment tab in the Format Cells dialog box, as shown in Figure 8.4.

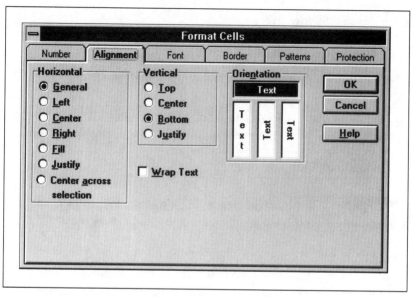

FIGURE 8.4: *The Alignment tab in the Format Cells dialog box*

4. Choose a horizontal option.
5. Select **OK** in the Format Cells dialog box.

• • • **Wrapping and Justifying Text**

If you type more text in a cell than will fit, the text appears to be in adjacent cells. If you type **Quarterly Data for 1995** in A1, it appears to be in B1 and C1, also. Now select B1 and type **Qtr 1**. Most of the characters in A1 seem to disappear. You can *wrap* the text in A1 so it reappears on your screen. Wrapped text flows to the next horizontal line in a cell.

TIP *You can also adjust the column width to display all of the text in a cell. Chapter 7 contains information on changing the width of a column.*

To wrap text, follow these steps:

1. Select the cell whose text you want to wrap.

2. Right-click on the selected cell, then choose Format Cells from the shortcut menu.

3. If necessary, click on the Alignment tab.

4. Click on the Wrap Text check box to select it.

5. Press ⏎ or click **OK**.

NOTE *Text that is not displayed on your screen because it will not fit in a cell is not printed when you print the document.*

Notice in Figure 8.5 that the heights of A1 and all the cells in row 1 were automatically changed to accommodate the wrapped text in that cell.

To automatically wrap and *justify* (align text along both the right and left edges of the cell) text in a cell, select the Justify option button in the Horizontal area of the Alignment tab instead of the Wrap Text check box.

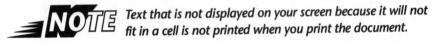

FIGURE 8.5: *When text is wrapped in a cell, Excel automatically adjusts the height of the cell.*

···Copying Formats with the Format Painter

One of the new features in Excel 5.0 is the *Format Painter,* located on the Standard toolbar. Click on **Format Painter** to copy formats in selected cells to another cell.

> **NOTE** *If you double-click on the* Format Painter *button, you can copy the selected format to several locations. When you are finished, click on the button again or press* Esc.

1. Select a cell that contains data with the format you want to apply.

2. Click on the **Format Painter** button. When you move the mouse pointer into the worksheet grid, it appears as a three-dimensional plus sign with a paintbrush.

3. Click on the cell or drag through the range to which you want to copy the selected format.

Printing Your Data

● ● ● ● ● ● *fast track*

To choose options for printing the active worksheet, select File ➤ Page Setup.

To display the worksheet as it will appear when printed, click **Print Preview** on the Standard toolbar.

To print the worksheet using the current print settings, click **Print** on the Standard toolbar.

THIS chapter tells you how to set up a Windows printer and choose options for printing a worksheet. It also explains how to easily change Excel's default printing options.

... **Setting Up the Printer**

Before you can print in Windows, you must select the printer that will be used.

NOTE *Any time you set up a printer in Windows, it becomes the default printer until you set up a different printer. For example, if you set up a printer in Word for Windows, Excel will use the same printer until you choose a different one.*

1. Select File ➤ Print (**Ctrl+P**) to display the Print dialog box, as shown in Figure 9.1.

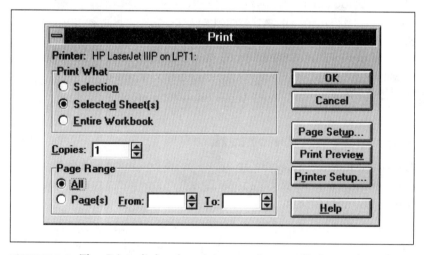

FIGURE 9.1: *The Print dialog box lets you choose all the options for printing your worksheet.*

2. Click on **Printer Setup** to display the Printer Setup dialog box.

3. Select the printer you want to use in the Printer list box.

4. Select **OK** in the Printer Setup dialog box.

5. Choose **OK** in the Print dialog box to print, or **Cancel** to return to the worksheet.

... Designing the Page

Once you set up a printer, you can choose several options to enhance the appearance of your printed worksheet.

 *The default page design options are used to print every workbook. Options you change are saved only in the active workbook file.*

Use the Page Setup dialog box to change any of the page design options. To display the dialog box, select File ➤ Page Setup.

*You can also display the Page Setup dialog box by clicking on **Page Setup** in the Print dialog box.*

Changing the Orientation

On the Page tab, select Portrait to print on a page that is longer than it is wide or Landscape to print on a page that is wider than it is long.

Select another tab to change more page design options, or click **OK** in the Page Setup dialog box to return to your worksheet.

Setting the Margins

You can change the page margins as needed to accommodate different sized worksheets.

1. Select the Margins tab in the Page Setup dialog box to display the options shown in Figure 9.2.

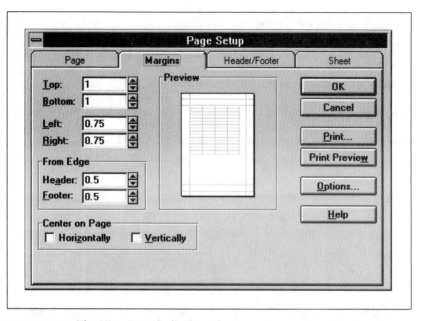

FIGURE 9.2: *The Margins tab displays the current margin settings.*

2. Type the measurement (in inches) you want for the Top, Bottom, Left, and Right margins in the corresponding text box.

3. In the Header and Footer text boxes, type the distance (from the top of the page) where you want the header to appear and (from the bottom of the page) where you want the footer to appear.

4. Select the Horizontally check box to center the data horizontally and the Vertically check box to center the data vertically on the page.

5. Click on another tab to choose additional options or choose **OK** to return to the worksheet window.

Adding Headers and Footers

Excel comes with several built-in headers and footers you can select for the active workbook, or you can create a custom header or footer.

1. Click on the Header/Footer tab in the Page Setup dialog box.

2. To select a built-in header or footer, select the Header or Footer drop-down list, then select one of the built-in headers or footers in the list.

3. To create a custom header or footer, click Custom Header or Custom Footer. The corresponding dialog box appears, similar to Figure 9.3. Choose the items to insert and type any text for the header or footer, then select **OK**.

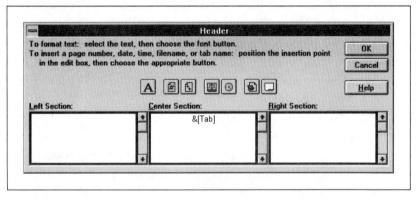

FIGURE 9.3: *Use this dialog box to add and format text and choose other options for a customized header or footer.*

The section text boxes indicate where the text or other item appears in the header or footer. Click on any of the buttons above the section text boxes to insert the corresponding item at the position of the insertion point. The buttons allow you format selected text or insert a page number, the total number of pages, the date and time, and the name of the file or sheet.

4. Select another tab in the Page Setup dialog box or choose
OK to return to your worksheet.

Choosing What to Print

The options you select on the Sheet tab of the Page Setup dialog box determine which parts of the active worksheet will be
printed.

1. Select the Sheet tab, shown in Figure 9.4, in the Page
Setup dialog box.

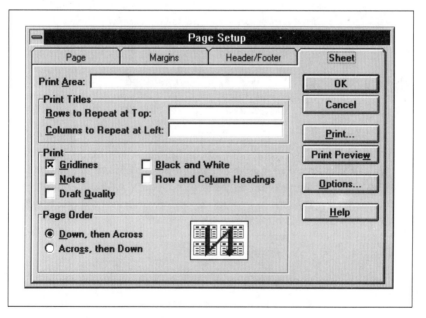

FIGURE 9.4: *Choose what will actually be printed on the Sheet tab of the
Page Setup dialog box.*

2. Type the cell references or range names you always want
to print in the Print Area text box.

3. Type the references or ranges of the titles for each page in the Rows to Repeat at Top and Columns to Repeat at Left text boxes.

4. Clear the Gridlines check box in the Print area so the worksheet's gridlines will not appear on the printed page.

5. Choose Down, then Across or Across, then Down to define the order of the printed pages.

6. Select **OK** in the Page Setup dialog box or select another tab to change other page design options.

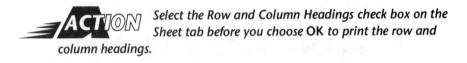 *Select the Row and Column Headings check box on the Sheet tab before you choose OK to print the row and column headings.*

• • • Previewing Your Document

Before you print the worksheet, display it in Print Preview mode so you can see how it will appear when you print it.

Previewing your document will save time you might otherwise spend making trips to the printer to reprint the document after adjusting your design options or printing a draft copy of a worksheet to see how it will appear.

To switch to Print Preview mode:

- Click the **Print Preview** button on the Standard toolbar while you are in the worksheet window.
- Select File ➤ Print Preview.
- Select Print Preview in the Print dialog box.
- Choose Print Preview in the Page Setup dialog box.

When you are in Print Preview mode, Excel displays the active worksheet and the Print Preview toolbar, similar to Figure 9.5.

FIGURE 9.5: *The Print Preview toolbar appears in Print Preview mode.*

Use any of the following methods to adjust the page design in Print Preview mode:

- Select **Next** (**N**) to display the next printed page of the worksheet.

- Select **Previous** (**P**) to display the preceding printed page.

- Select **Zoom** (**Z**) to magnify the displayed page. Select **Zoom** again to reduce the page.

- Choose **Setup** (**S**) to display the Page Setup dialog box.

- The **Margins** (**M**) button toggles the display of the margin and column-width handles. Drag a handle to change its corresponding measurement.

- When you are finished previewing your document, select **Close** (**C**) to return to your worksheet.

• • • Printing a Worksheet

To print a worksheet:

- Click **Print** on the Standard toolbar in the worksheet window.

- Select **Print** (**T**) in Print Preview mode, then choose **OK** in the Print dialog box.

- Select File ➤ Print (**Ctrl+P**), then choose **OK** in the Print dialog box.

- Select Print in the Page Setup dialog box and choose **OK** in the Print dialog box.

Changing the Display

IN this chapter, you will learn how to change the way Excel displays your worksheet. You will see how to add color to a worksheet, display formulas instead of results in cells, or freeze column and row titles.

··· Changing Display Options

Excel's display options appear on the View tab in the Options dialog box. To change what is displayed on the current worksheet, select Tools ➤ Options, then click on the View tab, which appears in Figure 10.1.

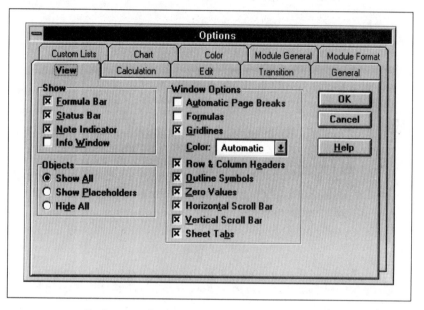

FIGURE 10.1: *Options on the View tab allow you to change the display.*

- Clear the Gridlines check box to hide the worksheet's gridlines. Hidden gridlines are not printed when you print the worksheet.

- To change the color of gridlines, select the Gridlines check box, then select a color in the Color drop-down list.

- Select the Formulas check box to display formulas in cells instead of their results, double the width of each column, and left-align each cell's contents in the active worksheet.

- To remove row and column headings, clear the Row & Column Headers check box.

- To display more of the current worksheet, clear the Horizontal Scroll Bar and Vertical Scroll Bar check boxes.

- To always display more of a worksheet, clear the Formula Bar and Status Bar check boxes.

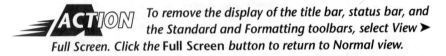 *To remove the display of the title bar, status bar, and the Standard and Formatting toolbars, select View ➤ Full Screen. Click the* **Full Screen** *button to return to Normal view.*

Select **OK** in the Options dialog box to put your changes into effect.

••• Changing the Colors

To change the color of characters in selected cells, click on the **Font Color** drop-down button on the Formatting toolbar, then choose a color in the palette.

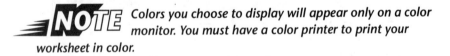 *Colors you choose to display will appear only on a color monitor. You must have a color printer to print your worksheet in color.*

Click the **Color** drop-down button on the Formatting toolbar to display your choices for adding a color to the background of all selected cells. Then click on the color in the palette that appears.

 *You can drag either palette off the toolbar to display it on your screen as you change the worksheet's display.*

• • • **Freezing Panes in the Worksheet**

Freeze the titles on your worksheet so that when you scroll through data, the titles remain displayed on your screen.

Select the cell just below the titles in the row and to the right of the titles in the column you want to freeze. For example, if your worksheet titles are in row 1 and Column A, select B2. Then select Window ➤ Freeze Panes. A border appears to indicate which cells are frozen, as shown in Figure 10.2.

	A	B	C	D	E	F	G
1		January	February	March	April	Qtr. 1 Total	
2							
3	Rent	$1,200.00	$1,200.00	$1,200.00	$1,200.00		
4	Insurance	$325.00	$325.00	$325.00	$325.00		
5	Telephone	$130.00	$130.00	$130.00	$130.00		
6	Postage	$100.00	$100.00	$100.00	$100.00		
7							
8	TOTAL						
9							

FIGURE 10.2: *A thin border appears to indicate frozen cells.*

Select Window ➤ Unfreeze Panes to release the frozen cells.

• • • **Splitting the Active Window**

Split the window of a large worksheet into two or four panes so you can still display titles as you scroll. You can use Window ➤ Split or the horizontal and vertical split boxes to split a worksheet.

NOTE *The horizontal split box is the solid black rectangle above the vertical scroll bar. The vertical split box is the solid black rectangle to the right of the horizontal scroll bar.*

- Select a row where you want to create a horizontal split, then choose Window ➤ Split or double-click on the horizontal split box. Two panes are created, as shown in Figure 10.3.

	A	B	C	D	E	F	G
1		January	February	March	April	Qtr. 1 Total	
2							
3	Rent	$1,200.00	$1,200.00	$1,200.00	$1,200.00	$4,800.00	
4	Insurance	$325.00	$325.00	$325.00	$325.00	$1,300.00	
5	Telephone	$130.00	$130.00	$130.00	$130.00	$520.00	
6	Postage	$100.00	$100.00	$100.00	$100.00	$400.00	
7							
8	TOTAL	$1,755.00	$1,755.00	$1,755.00	$1,755.00	$7,020.00	
9							
10	Office Supplies	$500.00	$500.00	$500.00	$500.00	$2,000.00	
11	Furniture	$600.00	$600.00	$600.00	$600.00	$2,400.00	
12	Equipment	$1,400.00	$1,400.00	$1,400.00	$1,400.00	$5,600.00	
13							
14	TOTAL	$2,500.00	$2,500.00	$2,500.00	$2,500.00	$10,000.00	
15	GRAND TOTAL						
16							

FIGURE 10.3: *Create two panes in a worksheet.*

- Select a column where you want to create a vertical split, then choose Window ➤ Split or double-click on the vertical split box.

- Select a cell where you want to create both horizontal and vertical splits, then choose Window ➤ Split or double-click on both the horizontal and vertical split boxes. Four panes are created, as shown in Figure 10.4.

To remove a split, double-click on the split bar or the split box, or choose Window ➤ Remove Split.

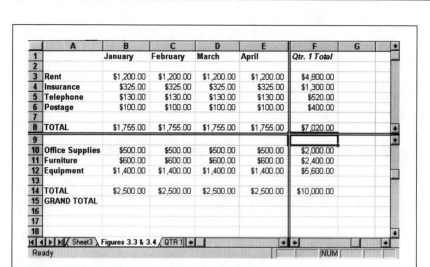

FIGURE 10.4: *Create four panes in a worksheet.*

Creating and Using Macros

•••••• fast track

To record a new macro, choose Tools ➤
Record Macro ➤ Record New Macro.

To run a macro, press **Ctrl+** the assigned
shortcut key.

To run a macro, choose Tools ➤ Macro, select
the macro, then select Run.

MACROS are groups of commands or keystrokes used to perform a task. Record a *macro* to automate a task you perform
often, then play back the macro to perform the task.

• • • **Recording a Macro**

Use Excel's Macro Recorder to record a macro. Each keystroke or selection with the mouse is recorded, including mistakes. By default, macros are stored in the workbook in which they were created.

> **TIP** *Select cells or objects before you record a macro so it will apply to your selection rather than a specific cell when you run the macro.*

1. Select Tools ➤ Record Macro ➤ Record New Macro to display the Record New Macro dialog box, shown in Figure 11.1.

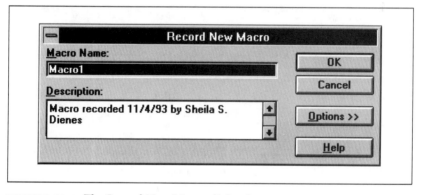

FIGURE 11.1: *The Record New Macro dialog box*

2. Type a name for the macro in the Macro Name text box.

3. Type a description of the macro in the Description text box.

4. Select **OK**. The **Stop Recording** button appears in its own toolbar.

5. Select the commands or type the keystrokes you want to record.

6. Click on the **Stop Recording** button or choose Tools ➤ Record Macro ➤ Stop Recording.

ACTION
Display the Visual Basic toolbar, then choose the Record Macro button to display the Record New Macro dialog box. See Chapter 12 for information on displaying toolbars.

A macro name can contain letters, numbers, and underscores, but cannot contain spaces or punctuation marks. Excel automatically names and describes each macro you record. However, you may want to replace the name and description with something more meaningful.

⋯ Creating a Personal Macro Workbook

Instead of saving your macros in the workbook where they were recorded, create a *Personal Macro Workbook* when you record a new macro. The Personal Macro Workbook is a hidden workbook controlled by Excel. It is always open, so macros you assign to it are available for any workbook.

NOTE
When you exit Excel correctly, you are automatically asked if you want to save changes to the Personal Macro Workbook when you store a new macro or edit an existing macro in it.

1. To assign a macro to the Personal Macro Workbook, select Options in the Record New Macro dialog box. The dialog box expands, as shown in Figure 11.2.

2. Select Personal Macro Workbook in the Store in area of the dialog box.

3. Choose **OK**.

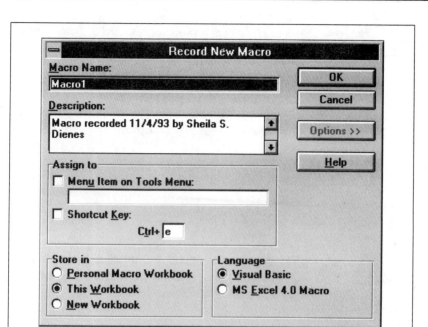

FIGURE 11.2: *Select Options to expand the Record New Macro dialog box.*

To display the Personal Macro Workbook, select Work-book ➤ Unhide, choose PERSONAL.XLS in the Unhide Workbook list box, then select OK.

All new macros are stored in the hidden workbook until you choose a different storage location.

··· Running a Macro

The workbook where the macro you want to run is stored must be open before you can run the macro.

 By default, each new macro is assigned a shortcut key. Press **Ctrl+** the assigned key to run a macro you have recorded.

To run (play back) a macro:

1. Choose Tools ➤ Macro. The Macro dialog box appears, similar to Figure 11.3.

2. Select the name of the macro in the Macro Name/Reference list box.

3. Select **Run**.

 If you displayed the Visual Basic toolbar, click on the Run Macro *button to display the Macro dialog box,* then highlight the macro in the list box and select **Run**.

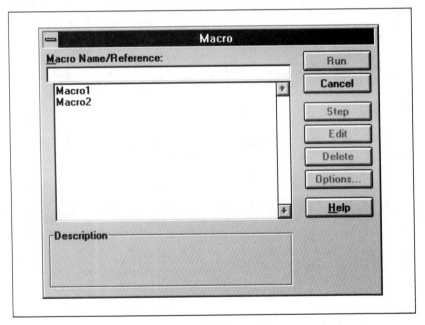

FIGURE 11.3: *The Macro dialog box contains a list of available macros.*

Using the Toolbars

• • • • • • *fast track*

To access a toolbar's shortcut menu, right-click on a displayed toolbar, then click on the name of the toolbar to display.

To move a toolbar, drag its background.

To move or copy a toolbar button, display the Toolbars or Customize dialog box.

THE Standard and Formatting toolbars are displayed by default in the worksheet window. You can create and display additional toolbars, or customize existing toolbars to suit your needs.

• • • **Tiptoe through the ToolTips**

Each time you move the mouse pointer onto a toolbar button or drop-down list, the *ToolTip* for that button appears just below the mouse pointer. The ToolTip is a brief description of the button's function. A slightly longer description of the button's function also appears in the Status bar.

• • • **Displaying Toolbars**

You can control which toolbars are displayed while you work in Excel.

1. Select View ➤ Toolbars to display the Toolbars dialog box, shown in Figure 12.1.

 *Right-click on one of the displayed toolbars to reveal the Toolbar shortcut menu, then click on the name of a toolbar you want to display. Displayed toolbars appear on the menu with a check mark beside their names.*

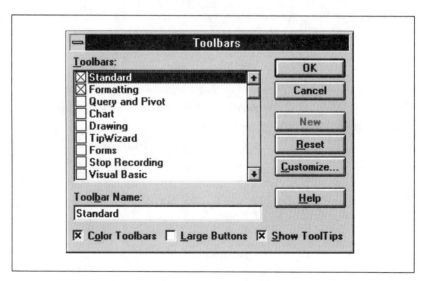

FIGURE 12.1: *Use the Toolbars dialog box to display additional toolbars.*

2. Select the check box of any toolbar you want to display in the Toolbars list box.

3. Choose **OK** to display the selected toolbars.

Moving a Toolbar

You can move Excel's toolbars anywhere on the screen. A toolbar placed on the worksheet is called a *floating* toolbar. Toolbars that appear along the edges of a worksheet are called *docked* toolbars. To move a toolbar, drag its background to a new location.

 *Double-click on the background of a toolbar to toggle it between a floating and docked toolbar.*

Floating toolbars are actually small windows, as shown in Figure 12.2. You can drag the title bar of a floating toolbar to move it to a different position, or click on its **Close** box to remove it from your screen. You can also change the size of a floating toolbar by dragging its border.

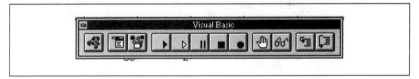

FIGURE 12.2: *Floating toolbars are actually small windows.*

If you drag a toolbar to the edge of the worksheet, it becomes docked. Docked toolbars are sized automatically, as shown in Figure 12.3.

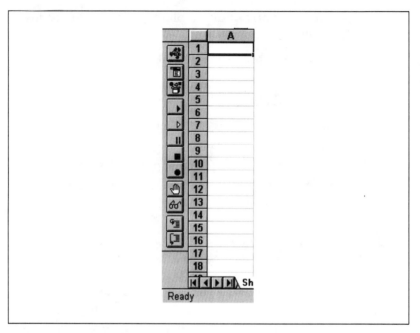

FIGURE 12.3: *Docked toolbars are automatically sized to fit along the edge of the worksheet.*

 *Toolbars that contain drop-down lists or palettes cannot be docked along the left or right edges of the window.*

• • • Customizing a Toolbar

Excel comes with many toolbar buttons that are not assigned to a specific toolbar. You can copy any button, whether it is assigned or not, to a displayed toolbar.

1. Select View ➤ Toolbars, then select Customize to display the Customize dialog box, shown in Figure 12.4.

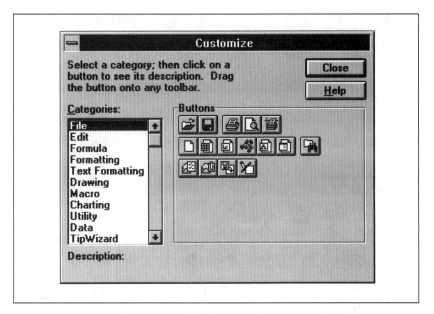

FIGURE 12.4: *Display the Customize dialog box to copy a toolbar button.*

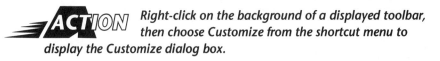 *Right-click on the background of a displayed toolbar, then choose Customize from the shortcut menu to display the Customize dialog box.*

2. Select the category that contains the button you want to copy in the Categories list box. The buttons for each category appear in the Buttons area.

3. Click on one of the displayed buttons. A description of its function appears in the Description area.

4. When you find the button you want to copy, drag it to the toolbar where you want it.

5. Repeat steps 2 through 4 as necessary.

6. Select Close in the Customize dialog box.

ACTION   *To restore the original buttons on one of Excel's built-in toolbars, select Toolbars from the shortcut menu to display the Toolbars dialog box. Then highlight the name of the toolbar in the Toolbars list box and select* **Reset**.

You can also move toolbar buttons from one toolbar to another. Display either the Toolbars or the Customize dialog box, then drag the button to a different displayed toolbar.

TIP   *To remove a button from a toolbar, drag it off the toolbar into the worksheet window while the Toolbars or Customize dialog box is displayed.*

• • • Creating a New Toolbar

You cannot rename a toolbar, so assign a permanent name to a toolbar you create. To create a new toolbar:

1. Right-click on the background of a displayed toolbar, then choose Toolbars from the shortcut menu to display the Toolbars dialog box.

ACTION   *Display the Customize dialog box, then drag the button you want to the worksheet window to create a toolbar named Toolbar n, where n is a number assigned by Excel.*

2. Type the name of the new toolbar in the Toolbar Name text box.

3. Select **New**. The Customize dialog box and a small, floating toolbar appear.

4. Drag the buttons you want from each category in the Customize dialog box to the new toolbar.

5. Choose **Close** in the Customize dialog box.

••• Deleting a Toolbar

To delete a toolbar you created, follow these steps:

1. Display the Toolbars dialog box.

2. Highlight the name of the toolbar in the Toolbars list box.

 *You cannot delete any of Excel's built-in toolbars.*

3. Select **Delete**.

4. Choose **OK**.

Working with Lists

USE a worksheet to organize associated data by rows into labeled columns in a *list*. Excel automatically identifies a list as a simple database, with the rows as *records* and the columns as *fields*.

· · · Creating a List

To take advantage of Excel's automatic list features, follow these rules when you create a list:

- Place each list in a separate worksheet. You can, however, store many lists on different sheets of a workbook.

- Position a list in a worksheet so there is at least one blank column and row between it and other data in the worksheet.

 *The column labels, called the* **header row,** *in the first row are part of the list, even though they are not items in the list.*

- Do not place essential data to the left or right of a list because it may be hidden when you filter the list.

 Put each list by itself in a separate worksheet, so you don't have to have to remember these rules!

To create a list:

1. Select a new worksheet tab in a workbook.

2. Enter the column labels in the first row of the list, then apply a different format to the labels.

3. Apply the same format for each cell in a column of the list. In Figure 13.1, each cell in column A is formatted with the *d-mmm-yy* date format.

 Do not insert a row of empty cells under the column labels in a list. To divide the column labels from the list items, add a solid border to the bottom edge of the cells that contain the labels.

4. Enter the data in the list without blank spaces at the beginning of each cell. Use uniform capitalization so you can sort the list later.

	A	B	C	D	E	F	G
1	DATE	QUANTITY	ITEM NO.	DESCRIPTION	COST	SALES TAX	TOTAL
2	2-Nov-93	100	1076	File folders	$5.50	$44.00	$594.00
3	28-Oct-92	150	1092	Pens, blue ballpoint	$7.00	$84.00	$1,134.00
4	6-Jan-94	75	2548	Rubber bands	$1.50	$9.00	$121.50
5	5-Nov-94	50	3673	Diskette labels	$12.00	$48.00	$648.00
6	14-Oct-93	175	2657	Pens, black ballpoint	$10.00	$140.00	$1,890.00
7	19-Dec-94	125	3429	Mailing labels	$18.00	$180.00	$2,430.00
8	17-Apr-95	200	4278	Pencils, No. 2	$2.00	$32.00	$432.00
9	18-Mar-94	125	3429	Mailing labels	$18.00	$180.00	$2,430.00
10	15-Apr-95	150	1092	Pens, blue ballpoint	$7.00	$84.00	$1,134.00
11	21-Jun-95	225	4278	Pencils, No. 2	$2.25	$40.50	$546.75
12	12-May-94	175	2657	Pens, black ballpoint	$10.00	$140.00	$1,890.00
13	16-Aug-95	100	1076	File folders	$5.50	$44.00	$594.00
14	28-Feb-94	75	2548	Rubber bands	$1.50	$9.00	$121.50
15	8-Mar-95	150	1092	Pens, blue ballpoint	$7.00	$84.00	$1,134.00
16							

FIGURE 13.1: *A sample Excel list*

5. Optionally, select the range of cells that contains the list, and choose Insert ➤ Name ➤ Define to define a name for the list.

••• Sorting Data

Once you have entered data in a list, you can organize it by columns alphabetically, numerically, or by date, by performing a *sort*. The rows of data in the list are rearranged according to the data in the column you chose to sort.

1. Select any cell in the list.

2. Choose Data ➤ Sort. Excel selects the entire list and displays the Sort dialog box, similar to Figure 13.2.

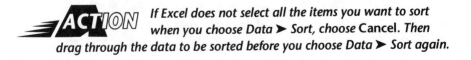

If Excel does not select all the items you want to sort when you choose Data ➤ Sort, choose Cancel. Then drag through the data to be sorted before you choose Data ➤ Sort again.

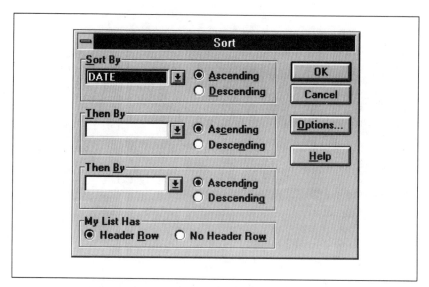

FIGURE 13.2: *Choose the label and the sort order for all items in the list.*

3. Select the Sort By drop-down list, then select the column label on which to sort the list. (To rearrange the data in Figure 13.1 by date, choose DATE.)

4. Select Ascending (A-Z) or Descending (Z-A) as the order in which the list will be sorted.

5. Choose **OK** in the Sort dialog box.

NOTE *Excel sorts the list by the column selected in the Sort By list box first, then sorts by the options selected in the first Then By area, and finally by the options in the second Then By area of the Sort dialog box.*

If Ascending is the sort order for the list items, the list is rearranged as shown in Figure 13.3.

You can also sort duplicate list items according to the case of the text.

	A	B	C	D	E	F	G
1	DATE	QUANTITY	ITEM NO.	DESCRIPTION	COST	SALES TAX	TOTAL
2	28-Oct-92	150	1092	Pens, blue ballpoint	$7.00	$140.00	$1,759.00
3	14-Oct-93	175	2657	Pens, black ballpoint	$10.00	$9.00	$153.00
4	2-Nov-93	100	1076	File folders	$5.50	$44.00	$594.00
5	6-Jan-94	75	2548	Rubber bands	$1.50	$44.00	$594.00
6	28-Feb-94	75	2548	Rubber bands	$1.50	$40.50	$590.25
7	18-Mar-94	125	3429	Mailing labels	$18.00	$48.00	$609.00
8	12-May-94	175	2657	Pens, black ballpoint	$10.00	$84.00	$1,230.00
9	5-Nov-94	50	3673	Diskette labels	$12.00	$9.00	$156.50
10	19-Dec-94	125	3429	Mailing labels	$18.00	$180.00	$2,298.00
11	8-Mar-95	150	1092	Pens, blue ballpoint	$7.00	$44.00	$582.00
12	15-Apr-95	150	1092	Pens, blue ballpoint	$7.00	$180.00	$2,430.00
13	17-Apr-95	200	4278	Pencils, No. 2	$2.00	$140.00	$1,834.00
14	21-Jun-95	225	4278	Pencils, No. 2	$2.25	$84.00	$1,094.00
15	16-Aug-95	100	1076	File folders	$5.50	$32.00	$540.00
16							

FIGURE 13.3: *Sorting the list.*

1. Select Data ➤ Sort to display the Sort dialog box.
2. Choose **Options**. The Sort Options dialog box appears, similar to Figure 13.4.
3. Select the Case Sensitive check box.
4. Choose **OK** in the Sort Options dialog box.
5. Choose **OK** in the Sort dialog box.

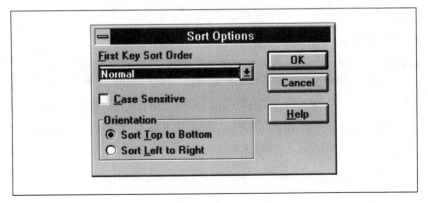

FIGURE 13.4: *The Sort Options dialog box lets you sort duplicate items by case.*

The sort order of duplicate items appears as all capitals, then initial capitals, and finally words in lowercase letters.

• • • **Filtering Data**

Use AutoFilter to display only the list items you choose from a column, called the *filter criterion*.

1. Select a cell in the list or select the labels for each column whose data you want to filter.

2. Choose Data ➤ Filter ➤ AutoFilter. A drop-down list arrow is assigned to each label (or each selected label) in the list, as shown in Figure 13.5.

	A	B	C	D	E	F	G
1	DATE	QUANTI	ITEM N	DESCRIPTION	COST	SALES TA	TOTAL
2	2-Nov-93	100	1076	File folders	$5.50	$44.00	$594.00
3	28-Oct-92	150	1092	Pens, blue ballpoint	$7.00	$84.00	$1,134.00
4	6-Jan-94	75	2548	Rubber bands	$1.50	$9.00	$121.50
5	5-Nov-94	50	3673	Diskette labels	$12.00	$48.00	$648.00
6	14-Oct-93	175	2657	Pens, black ballpoint	$10.00	$140.00	$1,890.00
7	19-Dec-94	125	3429	Mailing labels	$18.00	$180.00	$2,430.00
8	17-Apr-95	200	4278	Pencils, No. 2	$2.00	$32.00	$432.00
9	18-Mar-94	125	3429	Mailing labels	$18.00	$180.00	$2,430.00
10	15-Apr-95	150	1092	Pens, blue ballpoint	$7.00	$84.00	$1,134.00
11	21-Jun-95	225	4278	Pencils, No. 2	$2.25	$40.50	$546.75
12	12-May-94	175	2657	Pens, black ballpoint	$10.00	$140.00	$1,890.00
13	16-Aug-95	100	1076	File folders	$5.50	$44.00	$594.00
14	28-Feb-94	75	2548	Rubber bands	$1.50	$9.00	$121.50
15	8-Mar-95	150	1092	Pens, blue ballpoint	$7.00	$84.00	$1,134.00
16							

FIGURE 13.5: *A drop-down list appears by each column label when you are in Filter mode.*

3. Select the drop-down list of the column whose data you want to filter, then select the item to display.

4. If necessary, further filter the list by selecting another column's drop-down list, then selecting the item to display.

To manage a filtered list:

- Select the drop-down list for a column whose filter you want to remove, then choose All.

- Select Blank from the drop-down list of a column to display rows that contain empty cells in that column.

- Select Nonblank from the drop-down list of a column to display rows that contain data in the cells of that column.

- To redisplay all rows of a filtered list, select Data ➤ Filter ➤ Show All.

- To leave AutoFilter mode, select Data ➤ Filter ➤ AutoFilter.

• • • Creating a Data Form

Add or edit records directly in the list, or create a data form in a list named *DATABASE* to add new records or edit existing data.

1. Select a cell in the list.

2. Choose Data ➤ Form. The Form dialog box appears, similar to Figure 13.6.

3. To edit a specific record, select **Find Next** to display the next record or **Find Prev** to display the preceding record. Or drag the scroll box until the number of the record is displayed in the top-right corner.

4. To add a new record, select **New**, then type the information in each text box. Press **Tab** to move to the next text box.

5. When you are finished adding and editing records, select **Close**.

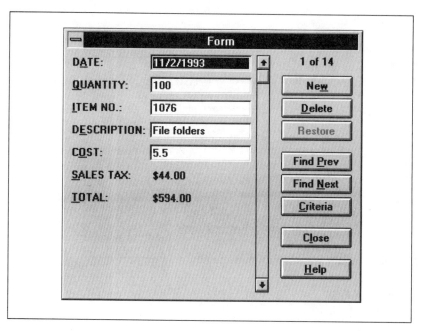

FIGURE 13.6: *The Form dialog box lets you edit existing records or enter new ones.*

· · · Adding Subtotals and Totals

Automatically subtotal and total or otherwise calculate a summary of groups of items in your list.

1. Sort the list so each group of items for which you want a summary appears together.

2. Choose Data ➤ Subtotals to display the Subtotal dialog box, similar to Figure 13.7.

3. Select the group to summarize in the At Each Change In drop-down list.

4. Select the function you want to use to calculate the summary in the Use Function drop-down list.

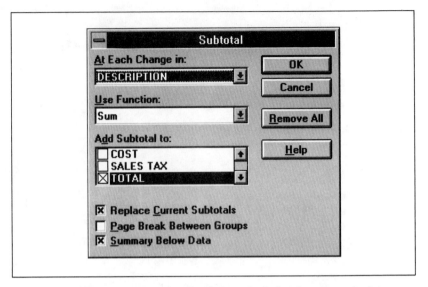

FIGURE 13.7: *Select options in the Subtotal dialog box to calculate a summary of the list.*

5. Select the check box for each column where the summary is to appear in the Add Subtotal To list box.

6. Choose **OK** in the Subtotal dialog box.

When you calculate a summary of your data, the worksheet appears as an outline. Use the outline to display and print only the summary information.

To remove the summary information from the list, follow these steps:

1. Select Data ➤ Subtotals.

2. Select Remove All in the Subtotal dialog box.

3. Choose **OK**.

Adding a Chart to a Workbook

• • • • • • fast track

To create an embedded chart, select the data you want to chart, then click on the **Chart-Wizard** button on the Standard toolbar and click in the worksheet.

To create a chart sheet, select the data you want to chart, then press **F11**.

To activate an embedded chart, click on it.

A *chart* is a picture of your data, displayed to make it easier to understand. You can create various types of charts in Excel to help you analyze or compare important data.

• • • Parts of a Chart

Charts consist of various parts. The parts of a two-dimensional chart are shown in Figure 14.1.

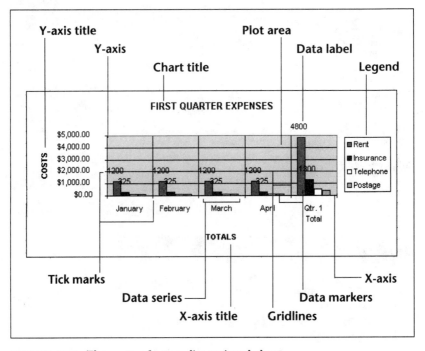

FIGURE 14.1: *The parts of a two dimensional chart*

Here is a description of the parts of a two-dimensional chart:

- The *X-axis* is the axis on which the categories are plotted.
- The *Y-axis* is where the values are plotted.
- The *X-axis title* is a short description of the categories.
- The *Y-axis title* is a short description of the values.
- The *data series* is the picture of the row or column of data used to plot points on the chart.
- A *data label* is the value of an individual data marker.
- Assign a *chart title* to name the chart.
- A symbol that displays a value is a *data marker*.

- The *legend* is an inset in the chart that defines the data markers.

- *Tick marks* are small lines that meet the axis and identify a category or data series.

- *Gridlines* begin at tick marks and continue horizontally or vertically through the chart.

- The *plot area* of the chart contains the gridlines, tick marks, and data series.

A three-dimensional chart, shown in Figure 14.2, has these additional parts:

- The *Z-axis* is the axis where the values are plotted.

- The *Y-axis* is where the data series appear on the chart.

- The *wall* of the chart displays the scale of the plotted values.

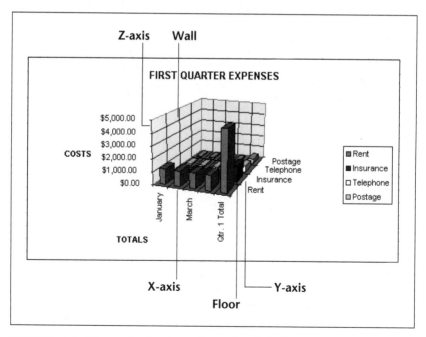

FIGURE 14.2: *The parts of a three-dimensional chart*

- The *floor* is the base of the chart (often representing the zero point).

● ● ● Creating a Chart with Chart Wizard

Excel's Chart Wizard takes you step by step through the creation of a chart. You can *embed* a chart on the same worksheet as your data (place the chart as a graphic object beside its data) or position a chart on a separate worksheet, called a *chart sheet*. An Excel chart is linked to the data in the cells you selected to create the chart.

 *An embedded chart is printed with the worksheet. A chart on a chart sheet is printed separately.*

To create a chart:

1. Select data in the worksheet you want to chart. You can select data in non-adjacent columns or rows.

2. Click on the **ChartWizard** button on the Standard toolbar. The mouse pointer changes into a crosshair with a small chart attached. If necessary, select a new worksheet tab.

ACTION To create a chart sheet, select the data then press **F11**. *A chart sheet is inserted directly before the sheet that contains the selected data, bypassing the ChartWizard.*

3. Click in the worksheet to automatically position the chart, or drag the crosshair to create a rectangle in which to place the chart. The ChartWizard - Step 1 of 5 dialog box appears, similar to Figure 14.3.

4. Make sure the data you selected appears in the Range text box, then select **Next**. The ChartWizard - Step 2 of 5 dialog box appears, as shown in Figure 14.4. Click on the kind of chart you want.

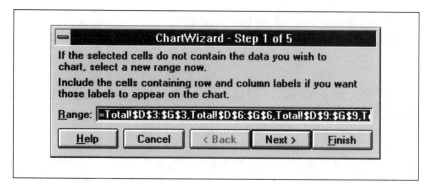

FIGURE 14.3: *The ChartWizard - Step 1 of 5 dialog box appears when you click on the ChartWizard button.*

5. Select **Next** to display the ChartWizard - Step 3 of 5 dialog box, then choose a format for the type of chart you selected in step 3.

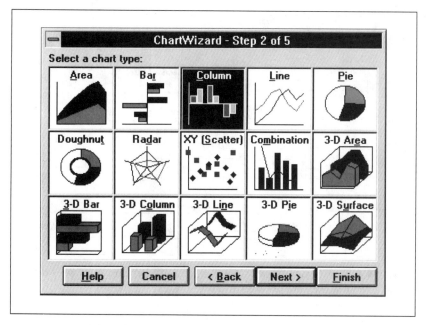

FIGURE 14.4: *Select the kind of chart you want for your data.*

6. Select **Next** to display the ChartWizard - Step 4 of 5 dialog box. If necessary, choose different options for the type of chart you selected in step 3.

NOTE *Select Finish at any time and edit the chart later, or select the Back or Next buttons to edit the chart text and format while you are in the Chart Wizard dialog box.*

7. Select **Next** to display the ChartWizard - Step 5 of 5 dialog box, shown in Figure 14.5. Choose Yes to add a legend to the chart, and type titles for each axis in the Category (X), Value (Y), and Second (Y) text boxes.

8. Select **Finish** to place the chart in the sheet.

TIP *Click on an embedded chart to select the entire chart. Drag just inside the border of a selected chart to move it. Drag one of the handles of a selected chart to change its size.*

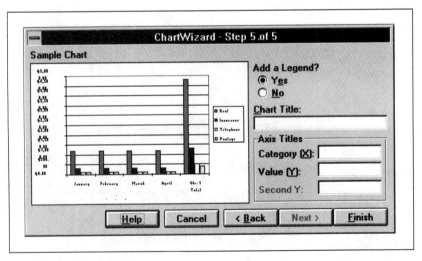

FIGURE 14.5: *The ChartWizard - Step 5 of 5 dialog box lets you add descriptive text to the chart.*

••• **Adding and Deleting Chart Data**

To change the data that was used to create a chart, edit it in the worksheet cells just as you would edit any data. Changes you make to data in the worksheet are automatically reflected in a chart created with that data.

••• **Adding and Editing Chart Text**

To add text to the chart:

1. Double-click on an embedded chart to activate it.

2. Right-click on an activated, embedded chart or on an item in a chart sheet to display its shortcut menu.

3. Select Insert Titles in the shortcut menu. The Titles dialog box appears, as in Figure 14.6.

4. Select the Chart Title, Value (Y) Axis, and Category (X) Axis check boxes.

5. Choose **OK**. The Titles dialog box disappears and a small, selected, text box containing an *X* appears at the bottom of the chart.

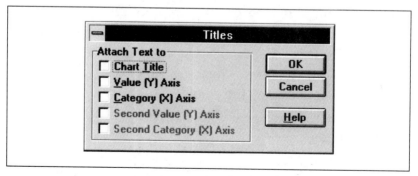

FIGURE 14.6: *The Title dialog box*

6. Type the text for the Category (X) Axis in the text box. Press ↵ to enter the text in the text box. The text box expands to accommodate all the text you entered.

7. Click on the *Y* that appears at the center-left edge of the chart, then type the text for the Value (Y) Axis and press ↵.

8. Click on *Title* at the top of the chart. Type the title text and press ↵.

9. Click in the worksheet or chart sheet to remove the handles from the selection.

To edit any of the text, click on the text to select its text box, then type new text and press ↵.

 *Right-click on various parts of an embedded chart to display the shortcut menu for that part of the chart.*

... Formatting a Chart

Use AutoFormat to change the format (or type) of a chart.

1. Double-click on an embedded chart, then right-click on the chart to display its shortcut menu, or right-click on a chart on a chart sheet.

2. Select AutoFormat. The AutoFormat dialog box appears, as in Figure 14.7.

3. In the Galleries list box, select the type of chart in which you want to display the data.

4. Click on the format for your chart in the Formats area of the dialog box.

5. Choose **OK**.

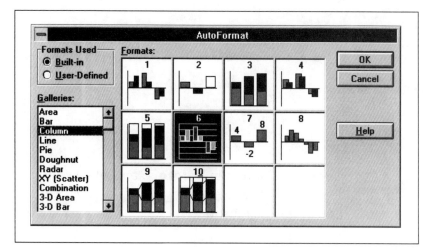

FIGURE 14.7: *Use AutoFormat to apply one of Excel's built-in formats to a chart.*

Index

About This Index Page numbers in **boldface** indicate definitions and principal discussions of primary topics and subtopics. Page numbers in *italics* indicate illustrations.

Symbols

, (comma) in reference operator names, 47
: (colon)
  in range names, 6–7
  in reference operator names, 47
$ (dollar sign)
  in absolute references, 42
  in mixed references, 43
= (equal sign) in formula names,
    17–18, 20
(number sign) in error value names, 19
( ) (parentheses)
  calculating formulas in, 19
  surrounding formulas with, 17

A

aligning data in cells, **56**, **60–61**
arguments, **20**
Arrange Windows dialog box, *39*
AutoFill, 9, **10–14**, 29
  copying data with, **12–13**
  shortcut menu, **13–14**
AutoFormat, **55**, **106–107**
AutoSum, **20–23**

B

boldface. *See* fonts
borders, adding, **49**, **53–55**

C

cell(s)
  aligning data, **56**, **60–61**
  applying borders, **49**
  changing the color, 72, **74**
  copying formatting, **56**
  deleting, **31–32**
  entering data in, **9–10**
  filling, **9**
  formatting, **56**
  inserting, **30–31**
  names, 41, **44–47**
  references, 5, **41–48**
changing color
  of cells, 72, **74**
  of characters in cells, **59**
  of characters in worksheets, **74**
chart(s), **99–107**
  adding text, **105–106**
  creating, 99, **102–104**

Tools ➤ Record Macro ➤ Stop Recording, 80
ToolTips, **4**, **84**

U

underlining. *See* fonts
undoing commands and actions, **30**
Unhide dialog box, *53*
Union operator, **47**

V

View ➤ Full Screen, 74
View ➤ Toolbars, 84, 86

W

walls, chart, **101**
Window ➤ Arrange, 38–39
Window ➤ Freeze Panes, 72, 75
Window ➤ Hide, 39
Window ➤ N, 39
Window ➤ New Window, 38
Window ➤ Remove Split, 76
Window ➤ Split, 75–76
Window ➤ UnFreeze Panes, 75
Window ➤ Unhide, 40
Windows, running, **1**
Workbook ➤ Unhide, 81
workbook(s), **33–40**. *See also*
    worksheet(s)
  adding charts, **99–107**
  adding sheets, **35**
  copying sheets, **36**
  creating, **9–16**
  deleting worksheets, **35**
  moving and copying sheets between,
    37
  moving around, **7–8**
  moving between sheets, **34–35**

moving sheets within, **36**
number of worksheets contained in, 33
opening files, **27–28**
opening windows, 1, **2–3**, **38–40**
renaming worksheets, **35**
saving, **14–15**
tabs, **5**
window elements, **3–4**
worksheet(s), **5**. *See also* workbook(s)
  activating, **33**
  changing the color of characters in, **74**
  changing the display, **72–77**
  copying, **33**, **37**
  copying data, **28–29**
  formatting, **49–55**
  freezing panes, **75**
  freezing titles, 72, **75**
  functions, **20–23**
  hiding, **53**
  inserting new, **33**
  moving around, **7–8**
  moving between, **34**
  moving data in, **28–29**
  names, 44–45
  printing active, **9**
  saving active, **9**
  selecting items, **6–7**
  splitting windows, 72, **75–76**
wrapping text, **61–62**

X

x-axes, **100**

Y

y-axes, **100–101**

Z

z-axes, **101**

··· **Excel's Toolbars** continued

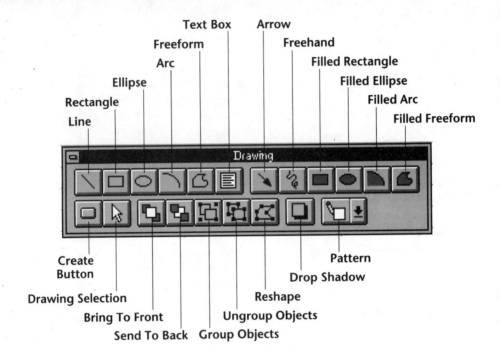

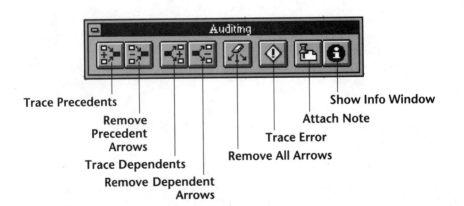